The Iranian Rentier State

Arash Duero

The Iranian Rentier State:

Rentierism, Political Stability and Economic Development in Iran

VDM Verlag Dr. Müller

Impressum/Imprint (nur für Deutschland/ only for Germany)
Bibliografische Information der Deutschen Nationalbibliothek: Die Deutsche Nationalbibliothek verzeichnet diese Publikation in der Deutschen Nationalbibliografie; detaillierte bibliografische Daten sind im Internet über http://dnb.d-nb.de abrufbar.

Coverbild: www.purestockx.com

Verlag: VDM Verlag Dr. Müller Aktiengesellschaft & Co. KG
Dudweiler Landstr. 99, 66123 Saarbrücken, Deutschland
Telefon +49 681 9100-698, Telefax +49 681 9100-988, Email: info@vdm-verlag.de

Herstellung in Deutschland:
Schaltungsdienst Lange o.H.G., Berlin
Books on Demand GmbH, Norderstedt
Reha GmbH, Saarbrücken
Amazon Distribution GmbH, Leipzig
ISBN: 978-3-639-14923-4

Imprint (only for USA, GB)
Bibliographic information published by the Deutsche Nationalbibliothek: The Deutsche Nationalbibliothek lists this publication in the Deutsche Nationalbibliografie; detailed bibliographic data are available in the Internet at http://dnb.d-nb.de.

Cover image: www.purestockx.com

Publisher:
VDM Verlag Dr. Müller Aktiengesellschaft & Co. KG
Dudweiler Landstr. 99, 66123 Saarbrücken, Germany
Phone +49 681 9100-698, Fax +49 681 9100-988, Email: info@vdm-verlag.de

Printed in the U.S.A.
Printed in the U.K. by (see last page)
ISBN: 978-3-639-14923-4

Table of Contents

List of Tables and Figures

Abbreviations

AIOC	Anglo-Iranian Oil Company
CIA	Central Intelligence Agency
Dh	Dirham
GDP	Gross domestic product
GNP	Gross national product
IAEA	International Atomic Energy Agency
ILSA	Iran-Libya Sanctions Act
IMF	International Monetary Fund
IR	Iranian rial
IRP	Islamic Republican Party
LNG	Liquefied natural gas
Mb/d	Million barrels per day
MKO	Mujahedin-e Khalq Organization
NIOC	National Iranian Oil Company
OPEC	Organization of Petroleum Exporting Countries
SIPRI	Stockholm International Peace Research Institute
UAE	United Arab Emirates (UAE)
WMD	Weapons of mass destruction

1. INTRODUCTION

The Islamic Republic of Iran (IRI) is one of the most populous and geo-politically significant countries in the Middle East. It shares land borders with several other important nations, including Afghanistan, Iraq, Turkey, India, Pakistan, Armenia, Azerbaijan and Turkmenistan. Its shorelines stretch along the Caspian Sea and the strategically vital Persian Gulf, a flow for 40% of the world's oil supply. Moreover, it is a leading energy producer richly endowed with vast oil and natural gas deposits, with the potential to greatly impact the international economy. Its unique form of government is the result of the only religious revolution in modern history and incorporates the tenets of Shia Islam into a representative and constitutional form of government. The year 2008 will mark the 29th anniversary of the Islamic Revolution in Iran, an event that catapulted the Islamic clerical establishment to power, brought about profound social and political changes domestically, and significantly impacted the geo-political and geo-economical dynamics of the international system, particularly that of the Middle East. For nearly thirty years the theocratic government in Tehran has managed to consolidate and centralize its power, cement its authority over the domestic populace, and exercise increasing influence in the Middle East and beyond; all this amidst an ever growing population that has nearly doubled over the past quarter century whilst its economic woes include a sharply increasing inflation rate, stagnant wage growth and a steadily shrinking economy characterized by a major decrease in real per capita income. Nevertheless, the government of the IRI has been able to maintain internal political control while simultaneously pursuing a more assertive foreign policy abroad. Economic sanctions, international isolation, and strict containment policies, in part initiated by the world's lone superpower, have apparently had little effect in weakening the theocracy in Tehran. It even managed to survive a debilitating, eight-year war with neighboring Iraq during the 1980's which depleted the state's coffers, devastated it's economic infrastructure, and cost an estimated 300,000 Iranians their lives. So what factor or factors have contributed to the Iranian state's resilience to sustain itself through times of political and economic shock?

1.1 Relevance

The importance of oil and gas to the world's economy is indispensable. It is the driving force of industry, transportation and modernization. Large oil companies have become a symbol of capitalist advancement and pure profit-generating entities wielding immense influence both in the corporate world and in global affairs. Inevitably, oil-rich states, being the source of these profits, have emerged as important international players that have been the focus of interest for many oil-importing nations. Some argue that resource-rich countries have been very fortunate, because energy export revenues have drastically added to the inflow of foreign cash, enabling such states to make record-breaking profits. Others, however, perceive the overabundance of oil as detrimental because it has prevented political change and stumped economic development. In any case, it is very difficult to overstate the importance of the analysis of economic variables and their role in influencing state behavior. Therefore, understanding the role of a state's economy and its interrelations with social and political structures is essential.

Currently, the IRI boasts the third largest reserves of conventional crude oil and the second largest gas reserves in the world.[1] It is the fourth largest oil producer and, as of 2006, produced roughly 5% of total global output.[2] Predictably, historically high oil and gas prices in 2006 and 2007 have considerably increased Iran's state revenues over the past few years, although new studies indicate that this trend is declining.[3] Invariably, oil and gas proceeds have been a huge source of income for the IRI. According to the Atieh Consulting Group, oil exports comprise about 75%-90% of the country's hard currency earnings. Many proponents of oil-led development would argue that the added profits should provide the Iranian state with the additional capacity needed to enhance economic growth and development, improve political and social infrastructures and reduce domestic poverty. [4]And yet,

---

[1] Statistical data varies minimally according to various sources including OPEC, the Oil and Gas Journal, BP, and the NIOC. The general consensus remains that, excluding non-conventional oil reserves, Iran, by any account, has the third largest proven oil reserves (after Saudi Arabia and Iraq) and the second largest gas reserves (after the Russian Federation) in the world.

[2] CIA World Factbook. May 2008. https://www.cia.gov/library/publications/the-world-factbook/geos/ir.html

[3]Associated Press. "Iran Revenue Quickly Drying Up, Analysis Says," in *Washington Post,* Dec. 26, 2006. http://www.washingtonpost.com/wp-dyn/content/article/2006/12/25/AR2006122500486.html

[4]"Oil-led development" is characterized by Terry Karl as development based on overwhelming dependence on revenues from the export (and not the internal consumption) of petroleum, as measured by the ratio of oil and gas to GDP, total exports, and the contribution to central government revenues. This definition will also be used for the purposes of this study.

despite current high global energy prices and the windfall of profits, Iran's economy has remained stagnant, poverty and unemployment levels are high, and few political changes and reforms have been undertaken to steer the nation away from a repressive and authoritarian form of government. Furthermore, the state's allocation of wealth from its oil revenues and the domestic redistribution of capital demonstrate a complex network of patronage and rent-seeking behavior that hints at all the characteristics of a rentier state.

1.2 Research Question

The study focuses on the Iranian rentier state and the political and economic impact rent-seeking has had after the Islamic Revolution of 1979; specifically, the rentier character and structure of the state as well as the domination of its economy by the petroleum sector will be elucidated. It is concerned with the rentier nature of Iran's oil-led, economic development and the role it has played in sustaining the authoritarian rule of the state over the past 29 years. It will identify rent-seeking behavior as one of the major causes of economic underdevelopment in Iran, while, at the same time, this behavior serves as a mechanism for the reinforcement and legitimization of its theocratic system of government. I will illustrate that, contrary to popular belief, a rentier system does not necessarily decrease the durability of authoritarian states. In fact, a rentier system can reinforce state structures, providing that such a state elects to first build effective institutions, strong coalitions, and undergo an initial power consolidation process that incorporates as many diverse social and political interest groups as possible. After the establishment of these state structures and institutions, I argue that a rentier system, through an extensive public sector, complex patronage networks, and wealth redistribution mechanisms, increases the domestic population's dependence on the state. Increased dependence on the state means that all actors involved (individuals, corporations, institutions, etc.) in a rentier economy have a greater vested interest in maintaining state stability, as it is the ultimate support structure of economic activity. What is more, I contend that two additional factors play a stabilizing role in the IRI: international isolation and external threats. The degree of international isolation has an impact on internal authoritarian stability. The more isolated Iran is, the more dependent does its' society become on the state to provide it with capital, employment, goods, services, information, raw materials, security, etc. External threats also play an important role in securing the power of authoritarian governments. In the IRI, these threats are instrumentalized by the state to unify the domestic population against a common enemy.

Figure 1: Contributing Factors to State Stability in the Islamic Republic of Iran

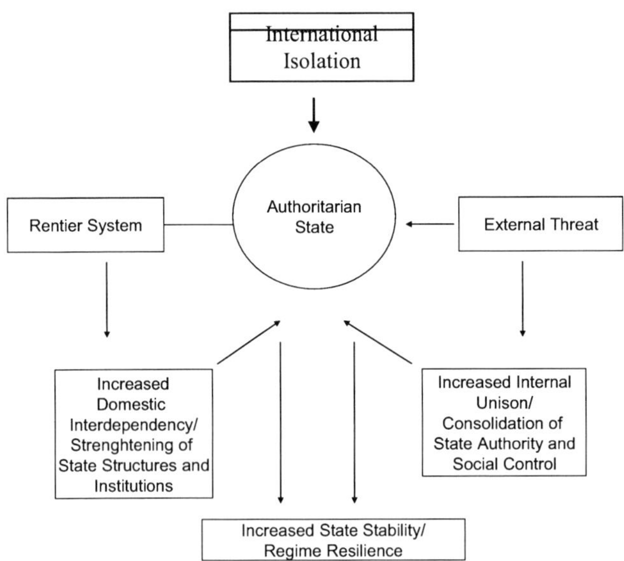

In the chapters that follow, I address the following questions:

1. What defines a "rentier state"?
2. What are the causes and consequences of rent-seeking activities in the IRI?
3. What role has oil-dependence played in the IRI?
4. What role do institutions play?
5. What reforms are necessary to make the economy more efficient?
6. How has the Iranian government utilized rent-seeking behavior to strengthen its own position domestically as well as internationally?
7. What factors contribute to the increase/decrease of authoritarian control?

In the first chapter, I offer a brief summary of the relevant existing literature on economic development. Subsequently, in chapter 2, I will outline the major theoretical conclusions of rentier theory and its usefulness for explaining economic underperformance in oil-dependent states. Chapter 3 very briefly traces the economic and political conditions in pre-revolutionary Iran leading up to the Islamic revolution of 1979. Chapters 4 through 7 present a case study of economic and political developments in the IRI, which are divided into four phases. The first phase (chapter 4) spans the time period between 1979-1988 and deals with the state and institution-building process directly after the revolution, the formation of an Islamic state, the eight-year Iran-Iraq war, and the political and economic policies of the Iranian ruling elite. Chapter 5 describes the second phase, taking place between 1988-1997, and focuses on the transition of power following the death of revolutionary leader Ayatollah Khomeini, the economic liberalization reforms undertaken by the pragmatic President Rafsanjani, and the political and economic impacts of his reforms on the IRI. The sixth chapter summarizes the third phase and the socio-economic liberalization reforms of President Mohammad Khatami. The social and political implications of his reforms will be discussed. The fourth and final phase, discussed in chapter 7, examines the presidency of Mahmoud Ahmadinejad and the new conservative agenda. Each chapter will analyze both economic and political developments in order to determine what factors contribute to regime stability or instability. In the conclusion (chapter 8), I summarize the results of this study and discuss the implications.

1.3 Literature: Theories of Economic Development

There are several theories and extensive literature that provide explanations for the problems associated with poor economic growth due to external rent dependency (particularly oil rent) and political stability/instability. Some argue that long-term political instability is the inevitable outcome of oil-led, developing states whereas others claim that the influx of foreign profits serves to strengthen authoritarian regimes. In the following section, I will briefly outline competing theories of economic development in order to examine the major arguments provided for the various causes of economic underdevelopment, external rent dependency, as well as political crises as a result of oil wealth. Additionally, this background information will serve to expound the role of rentier theory and its place in existing literature dealing with economic development.

Classical development economics is mainly concerned with the efficient and cost effective allocation of scarce resources and the optimal growth of those resources over time. This theory maintains that countries develop economically through the market and that economic benefits, reaped from self-interested and voluntary acts, are then transferred to various actors (i.e. companies, individuals, governments, countries). This behavior is utility-maximising, efficient and produces the most overall economic growth. It assumes that economic growth is beneficial to all even if the benefits are not always equally distributed. Proponents of this theory assert that the only obstacles that prevent sustained economic growth are "government-created barriers that restrict the free market."[5] Hence, in order "to stimulate growth, those inefficient barriers would have to be removed."[6]

The Marxist school of thought incorporates an additional, important factor into the traditional economic development theory, namely the role of politics. Political economists focus on factors such as social and political mechanisms that economic groups have created for the allotment of resources in order to explain problems and causes of poor economic growth, inequality and underdevelopment.
Contreras claims that "Marxism tends to be universally applied...for example, to an orthodox Marxist, the class struggle is a by-product of capitalism. Capitalism inevitably creates a conflict between the working class and the owners of capital. Regardless of the country in question, the conflict will always reach the same result: the social inequities will reach an intolerable point and the working class will instigate a socialist revolution that will overthrow the capitalist regime."[7] Marx states that "no social order ever disappears before all the productive forces, for which there is room in it, have been developed; and new higher relations of production never appear before the material conditions of their existence have matured in the womb of the old society."[8] In other words, in order for a social revolution to occur, a given state must first have undergone a capitalist transformation and have achieved an advanced stage of industrial development.[9] This line of argumentation is disputed by many

---

[5] Contreras, Ricardo. "Competing Theories of Economic Development," March 25, 2008. http://www.uiowa.edu/ifdebook/ebook2/contents/part1-III.shtml
[6] Ibid.
[7] Ibid.
[8] Reiss, David. „On the Theory of the Social Revolution Reconsideration of a Marxian Prediction," in *Marxist Internet Archive*, 2006. http://marx.org/history/international/comintern/sections/britain/periodicals/communist_review/1922/07/soc_rev.htm
[9] Marx, Karl, Engels, Friedrich and Tucker, Robert C.. *The Marx-Engels Reader.* Cambridge: Cambridge University Press, 1986.

scholars, even those who accept Marx's philosophy in principle. The latter, also known as neo-Marxists, claim that the Marxist paradigm is insufficient and has to be modified in order to explain underdevelopment in developing countries. They argue that, due to exploitation by the capitalist class and the inequality of exchange between industrialized nations and developing countries, the advanced stage of industrialization proposed by Marx can never be achieved, thus hindering social revolution. Neo-Marxists propose a different approach that analyzes the historical exploitation of developing nations by industrialized, capitalist states. "Marx's doctrine of surplus value stated that the worker was being robbed by the capitalist class. The worker received only a fraction of the value of the product which his labor produced. The difference was expropriated by the capitalists - the private owners of the factories and the machines;"[10] neo-Marxists lend this theory "an international dimension based on the behavior of nations."[11] They claim that by importing raw products at extremely low prices from developing countries and re-exporting finished products at much higher prices to the same states, developed countries are able to drastically increase their profit margins at the expense of developing countries, thus resulting in a state of continual poverty.

The Marxist view that economic and political power are heavily concentrated and centralized in industrialized, capitalist countries is, to an extent, shared by proponents of the dependency theory. But, whereas Marxism explains dominant state expansion, dependency theorists seek to explain the causes of underdevelopment. This school of thought, which is closely interlinked with neo-Marxist theory, shares three common features to its definition of dependency, namely[12]:

A. the international system is comprised of two spheres, variously described as dominant/dependent or center/periphery,

B. external forces (i.e. multinational corporations, international commodity markets, foreign assistance, communications, etc.) are extremely important to the economic activities of dependent states and

C. "that the relations between dominant and dependent states are dynamic because the interactions between the two sets of states tend to not only reinforce but also intensify the unequal patterns."[13]

---

[10] Contreras, Ricardo. "Competing Theories of Economic Development," March 25, 2008. http://www.uiowa.edu/ifdebook/ebook2/contents/part1-III.shtml

[11] Ibid.

[12] See: Ferraro, Vincent. „Dependency Theory: An Introduction. " July, 1996.

[13] Ferraro, Vincent. „Dependency Theory: An Introduction. " July, 1996.

Moreover, it assumes "the existence of a capitalist "world-system"" that is conceptually divided into two concentric spheres: an advanced capitalist core and an underdeveloped periphery. The relationship between the core and the periphery serves to impoverish the former and enrich the latter, so that the peripheral countries have been "underdeveloped" (in the active sense) by the same core states upon which they depended."[14] The underdeveloped peripheral states (oil-exporting) are usually exploited by the rich core states (oil-importing), thus resulting in conditions of dependency and stagnant economic growth. As a consequence, the dependency of the peripheral states on core states is the very cause of their underdevelopment. This theory has proven to be useful in explaining patterns and problems of development in economies heavily dependent on oil or hydrocarbon resources. Dissidents, on the other hand, contend that it fails to account for the formation of recently developed states that have emerged from the periphery of the world system.

Scholars of the "dependent development" school include Peter Evans and Fernando Cardoso, who challenge the notion that dependency necessarily generates underdevelopment. They agree that the current model of Western capitalism has created conditions of "dependency", but argue that capital formation through multinational corporations, other capital investments and financial aid have actually stimulated economic development, rather than hindered it. Peter Evans, for instance, cites Brazil as a prime example of such a state. He claims that the intense economic exchange between the state, multinational corporations and local capitalists, also termed as a "triple-alliance", has proven to be mutually beneficial. Whereas industrialized nations profit from the import of cheap primary products, developing states, in turn, can modernize various sectors of their economy through technological advancements imported from developed states. The challenge that remains for this "triple-alliance" is "...how the advances made by a "triple alliance" can be generalized, consolidated and improved."[15]

Although each of these developmental theories elucidate problems of dependency and underdevelopment in developing states to a certain extent, they also demonstrate difficulties when attempting to explain the specific case of underdevelopment/development in oil-rich states. There are several oil-rich states in

---

http://www.mtholyoke.edu/acad/intrel/depend.htm

[14] Yates, Douglas. *The Rentier State in Africa*. Trenton, N.J.: Africa World Press, 1996, p. 3.

[15] Ibid., p.4.

the Middle East that challenge the notion of these theories. Theories of dependence and underdevelopment put forth by Marxists, neo-Marxists, and dependency theorists fail to adequately explain why a contemporary, petroleum-dependent Gulf state such as the United Arab Emirates (UAE) has managed to accumulate immense wealth while simultaneously taking steps to diversify and modernize its economy in order to ensure long-term growth and development. If the goal of advanced capitalist states is to exploit and thwart development in underdeveloped states while enriching themselves in the process, then why has this not been the case here? For instance, although the UAE is still heavily dependent on petroleum and natural gas exports, it has managed to diversify its economy by expanding both the service and industrial sectors. A noticeable sectoral shift and contribution to GDP is evident in diverse sectors such as service, commerce, transport, storage, communications, finance, insurance, and real estate.[16] "The service sector contribution to GDP increased from 22.3 per cent in 1975 to 39.7 per cent in 1998."[17] In addition, industrialization in the UAE has broadened the base of the economy, as demonstrated by an increase in industrial productivity. Important factors such as an "...abundance of natural mineral resources, the ready availability of financial capital, a well-established infrastructure, a flexible labour and employment policy, the availability of cheap energy, industrial zones and various incentives in legislation, plus political and social stability"[18] have significantly advanced the UAE's industrial sector. "The value of industrial exports rose from Dh 11 million in 1975 to Dh 539 million in 1980, Dh 4825 million in 1985, and to Dh 8070 million in 1990 (in constant prices)."[19] Scholars of the "dependent development" school of thought also fail to account for states that have been dependent on foreign revenues, but have not experienced "dependent development" in the process. Qatar, for instance, has been posting impressive economic growth numbers for some years now. "Real GDP expanded by 9.2% and 10.2% in 2005 and 2006, respectively, and the International Monetary Fund (IMF) is forecasting that the aggregate economic output will likely grow to about 14% in 2008. Furthermore, the IMF is expecting the oil sector to register a real growth rate of 18%."[20] The natural

---

[16] Shihab, Mohamed. "Economic Development in the UAE" in al Abed, Ibrahim and Hellyer, Peter (ed.) *The United Arab Emirates: A New Perspective*. Trident Press, 2001, p. 253.
[17] Ibid.
[18] Ibid, p.254.
[19] Ibid, p.255.
[20] *Qatar Country Report 2007*, p.2.
www.bayernlb.de/ar/Internet/en/Downloads/0100_CorporateCenter/5700Countries/CountriesL-Z/Qatar/E-Qatar.pdf

gas and oil sectors claim the lion's share of Qatar's GDP, amounting to about 60%, and generating almost 90% of export revenues. With an estimated 15 billion barrels of proven oil reserves[21], the third-largest gas reserves worldwide, and being the largest producer of liquefied natural gas (LNG), Qatar's "share of the natural-gas industry in aggregate economic output is poised to become even larger in the years ahead."[22] In spite of its diversification efforts, the importance and priority given to its booming hydrocarbon industry has resulted in the underdevelopment of Qatar's other economic sectors.[23] Economic growth measured by cash-profits and wealth accumulation is therefore not always an accurate indicator of the state of a country's economic development, especially if various sectors of the economy do not experience commensurate development.

A more useful theory for the purposes of this study is the theory of the rentier state, which places special focus on patterns and problems of development in oil-dependent states. This theory claims "that the conditioning factor of economic stagnation and political authoritarianism in oil-dependent states is the corrosive effect of external rent. Rentier theory is as concerned with internal developments (such as the emergence of a rentier mentality and rentier class) as with external."[24] I adopt Beblawi's and Luciani's concept of the state which is defined as "the combination of essential indicators describing the relationship between the state and the economy."[25] Furthermore, the terms "rent" and "rentier state" need clarification. Because of the significant influence oil production and oil revenues have on the nature of the state, the term "rent" is here attributed to the oil revenues that constitute the major source of income for oil-exporting states.[26] Giacomo Luciani elaborates on the concept of the rentier state by delineating three clarifications to the concept. First, "there are other

---

21 *BP Statistical Review of World Energy Full Report 2007* http://www.bp.com/liveassets/bp_internet/globalbp/globalbp_uk_english/reports_and_publications/statistical_energy_review_2007/STAGING/local_assets/downloads/pdf/statistical_review_of_world_energy_full_report_2007.pdf

22 *Qatar Country Report* 2007, p.2. www.bayernlb.de/ar/Internet/en/Downloads/0100_CorporateCenter/5700Countries/CountriesL-Z/Qatar/E-Qatar.pdf

23 Increased output and demand of Qatar's hydrocarbon resources, especially LNG, will require substantial investments in the petrochemical and refinery sectors. This would, in effect reduce the amount of available financial investments for alternative sectors such as service and manufacturing. According to the Bayern LB Bank, a new investment law is on the economic agenda in order to increase the accessibility of other sectors of the economy to foreign investors.

24 Yates, Douglas. *The Rentier State in Africa*. Trenton, N.J.: Africa World Press, 1996, p. 6.

25 Beblawi, Hazem and Giacomo Luciani.*The Rentier State. Vol.2, Nation, State and Integration in the Arab World.* London: Croom Helm, 1987, p.4.

26 Terry Karl defines rent as earnings in excess of all relevant costs, including the market rate of return on invested assets. They are the equivalent of what most non-economists consider to be monopoly profits.

rent-like sources of revenue which accrue directly to the state besides oil: thus rentier states are not necessarily oil exporting states." [27] Second, he asserts that states should not be labelled as rentier when "some important flows of income do not accrue directly to the state."[28] Finally, it is essential that "the income of the state not only be in the nature of a rent, but also be earned abroad; if it were earned domestically the nature of the state would not be substantially affected."[29] Because we are dealing with a country heavily dependent on hydrocarbon exports, for the purposes of this study, the term "rentier state" will be used to describe a state whose oil revenues: 1) constitute a *significant* portion of its income, 2) accrue directly to the state and 3) originate from an external source.[30] The next chapter shall provide an introduction to the roots and key elements of rentier theory with the purpose of providing a theoretical basis necessary for the subsequent analysis of the Iranian economy after 1979. Additionally the chapter will detail the role of the state, and the correlation between oil-wealth and regime resilience and stability.

---

[27] Beblawi, Hazem and Giacomo Luciani. *The Rentier State. Vol.2, Nation, State and Integration in the Arab World.* London: Croom Helm, 1987, p.68.
[28] Ibid.
[29] Ibid.
[30] Ibid.

2. THE THEORY OF THE RENTIER STATE

The rise of the economic and strategic importance of hydrocarbon-rich exporting states such as the UAE, Qatar, and the IRI has prompted a renewed interest in the concept of the rentier state. Rentier theory is based on the supposition that the source of economic stagnation, underdevelopment and political authoritarianism is the negative effect of external rent in oil-dependent states. Douglas Yates defines the theory of the rentier state as "a complex of associated ideas concerning the patterns of development and the nature of states in economies dominated by external rent."[31] This chapter intends to only briefly explore the economic concept of rent because, in purely economic terms, rent is perceived no more different than any other price or income. "No value judgement is implied, rent is an economic price or factor income like any other price."[32] However, social scientists and economists do make a clear distinction between "earned" income and effortless "accrued" rent."[33] In addition, pure economic approaches to the study of economic development are based on an abstract notion of the state and usually perceive it as a neutral and homogenous entity. Beblawi and Luciani argue that "while some authors are inclined to attribute to the state a more limited role than others, this role is, in any case, substantial. As a minimum, it consists of the provision for security and guarantee of law and order, the establishment of modern economic legislation, the management of money supply, the surveillance of fairness of markets and the creation of basic infrastructure. Economic development cannot occur if the state does not offer certain preconditions and create an appropriate legal and political environment."[34] Because this study is based on the assumption that the government of the IRI plays a key role in determining economic development in Iran, a political-economic approach is needed. The aim of this chapter is to provide a brief historical account of theories of economic rent and the rentier state, identify key components and arguments, and explain the relevance of the theory for this study.

---

[31] Douglas. *The Rentier State in Africa*. Trenton, N.J.: Africa World Press, 1996, p. 11.
[32] Beblawi, Hazem and Giacomo Luciani. *The Rentier State. Vol.2, Nation, State and Integration in the Arab World.* London: Croom Helm, 1987, p.49.
[33] Ibid, p.50.
[34] Ibid, p.3.

2.1 Economic Theories of Rent

David Ricardo, one of the founders of the Classical School of Economics defined economic rent on land as the value of "the difference in productivity between a given piece of land and the poorest, most costly piece of land producing the same goods under the same conditions."[35] Hence, in agricultural production, relatively fertile land that produces harvest at a lower cost (i.e. for labor, technology, etc.) than its sale price usually results in the collection of rent. Should the costs of production equal or exceed its sale price, as may occur on infertile land, then rent would be non-existent. This theory is also termed as the "differential rent theory" and reflects the difference between the fertility or location of agricultural land on the macro-economic scale.[36] Classical economics included both a value theory and distribution theory. The value of goods produced was thought to depend on the labor costs involved in producing them. The explanation of costs was also simultaneously the explanation of distribution. Thus, a landlord received rent, laborers received wages, and capitalist tenant farmers received returns on their investments. [37] Adam Smith differentiates between rent and other sources of income such as wages and profits, stating:

> "Rent enters into the composition of the price of commodities in a different way from wages and profit. High or low wages and profit are the causes of high or low price; high or low rent is the effect of it."[38]

Furthermore, rent is not only the income of landowners or capitalist property owners but can be a result of the possession of all natural resources.

Karl Marx expands Ricardo's definition by describing economic rent as the "income accruing to asset-owning classes after paying for the direct costs of production (wages, raw materials and the depreciation costs of machinery)."[39] The appropriation of economic rent by landowners and capitalists is based on their ownership of land or capital, respectively. Without these specific property rights

---

[35] University of Toronto, Dept. of Economics. "Ricardo; Economic Rent and Opportunity Cost," 2004, p.1. http://www.economics.utoronto.ca/munro5/ECONRENT.pdf

[36] See: Yates, Douglas. *The Rentier State in Africa*. Trenton, N.J.: Africa World Press, 1996, p. 16.

[37] Ricardo, David. 1821. *The Principles of Economy and Taxation*. London: Everyman's Library.

[38] Smith, Adam. *The wealth of nations* (1776). London: Everyman's Library, 1960, p.412.

[39] Khan, Mushtaq and Jomo Kwame Sundaram, eds. *Rents, Rent-Seeking and Economic Development: Theory and Evidence in Asia*. Cambridge: Cambridge University Press, 2000, p.64.

prevalent in capitalism, normal profits and rents would not exist.[40] Marx disagrees with the classical interpretation of rent being the result of differences in the location or physical and technical make-up of land/property. He makes a clear distinction between Ricardo's economic rent received by feudal landlords and rent received by capitalist property owners, claiming that the former notion is premised on the "use value" of commodities while the latter is based on the "exchange value". The "use value" of goods does not take into account the social implications associated with "exchange value" goods, in which human interaction and commodity trade are closely interlinked. "To Marx, rent is a social relation, reflective and derivative of historically specific property relations in the dominant mode of production."[41]

Alternative approaches seem to overlook political determinants in rents, whereas the Marxian approach is very interested in the impact class conflicts can have on determining the amount of rent and its distribution. Although economic rent can be damaging for growth, it is also indispensable. "What is damaging is its mis-allocation in unproductive expenditures or its excessive consumption by parasitic capitalist landlords."[42] Accordingly, the role of the state, often being responsible for the accruement and distribution of economic rent (especially external rent), is significant.

2.2 The Rentier State

The nationalization of the Anglo-Iranian Oil Company (AIOC) in 1951 by the populist Prime Minister Mohammed Mossadegh, and the ensuing period between 1951-56 demonstrated a marked difference in the "structure and sources of economic growth" as compared to the preceding decades. [43] Hossein Mahdavy made this observation in 1970 and proposed an approach concerned with the "causes, prerequisites, patterns and problems of economic development" within the framework of "pinpointing and explaining certain uniformities within a more limited time span and

[40] See: Khan, Mushtaq and Jomo Kwame Sundaram, eds. *Rents, Rent-Seeking and Economic Development: Theory and Evidence in Asia.* Cambridge: Cambridge University Press, 2000, p.64.
[41] Yates, Douglas. *The Rentier State in Africa*. Trenton, N.J.: Africa World Press, 1996, p. 19.
[42] See: Khan, Mushtaq and Jomo Kwame Sundaram, eds. *Rents, Rent-Seeking and Economic Development: Theory and Evidence in Asia.* Cambridge: Cambridge University Press, 2000, p.64.
[43] Mahdavy, Hossein. "The patterns and problems of economic development in rentier states: the case of Iran." In: *M. A. Cook (ed.), Studies in the Economic History of the Middle East.* London: Oxford University Press. 1970, p.428.

for a more limited area."[44] The nationalization and development of the Iranian petroleum sector in the 1950's, skyrocketing global demand and the resulting inflow of foreign profits transformed some oil-exporting countries like Iran into rentier states. Mahdavy defines the rentier state as "those countries that receive on a regular basis substantial amounts of external rent."[45] In this context, external rents are any "rentals paid by foreign individuals, concerns or governments to individuals, or concerns or governments of a given country."[46] Based on this premise, external rents can also include oil revenues received by foreign governments. According to Mahdavy, the stage at which a state can be labelled "rentier" is determined arbitrarily, although most rentier states demonstrate situations where "the effects of the oil sector are significant and yet the rest of the economy is not of secondary importance."[47] It is important to note that accrued oil rents and the priority given (by the state) to the domestic sector involved in oil production are, to a great extent, autonomous of other sectors of the economy. That is, the "inputs from the local economies-other than the raw materials-are insignificant."[48] The decades following Mahdavy's study on the rentier state in Iran witnessed the emergence of new oil states in the 1970's, characterized by record-breaking profits, an increasingly powerful and strategically important Organization of Petroleum Exporting Countries (OPEC) cartel, and the Arab oil embargo, which was imposed as a direct reaction to the Israeli-Palestinian conflict in 1973. Due to the significance and impact of the oil phenomenon on the role of the state and the international economy, scholars such as Hazem Beblawi and Giacomo Luciani revived the concept of the rentier state "for lack of better concepts to characterise the prominence of the oil economies in the Arab region."[49]

Mahdavy's definition focused solely on the role of the state in rentier states. Beblawi and Luciani, on the other hand, state that "to focus exclusively on the state, independently of the economy, and define as rentier any state that derives a substantial part of its revenue from foreign sources and under the form of rent" is "a

---

[44] Mahdavy, Hossein. "The patterns and problems of economic development in rentier states: the case of Iran." In: *M. A. Cook (ed.), Studies in the Economic History of the Middle East.* London: Oxford University Press. 1970, p.428.
[45] Ibid.
[46] Ibid.
[47] Ibid, p.431.
[48] Ibid.
.See also: Issawi, Charles and Yeganeh, Mohammed. *The Economics of Middle Eastern oil.* London, 1962, pp. 105-6 and Table 30.
[49] Beblawi, Hazem and Giacomo Luciani. *The Rentier State. Vol.2, Nation, State and Integration in the Arab World.* London: Croom Helm, 1987, p.50.

rather restrictive definition that says little about the economy."[50] Instead, they propose an alternative concept that puts greater emphasis on the economy. This "rentier economy" is defined as an economy that is reliant on state expenditure, while the state itself is dependent on external rent. Furthermore, the state is not perceived to be synonymous with society as Mahdavy's definition of the rentier state implied; the state is defined as a "combination of essential indicators describing the relationship between the state and the economy."[51] Based on this assumption, the rentier state is categorized as a "sub-system associated with a rentier economy."[52] Thus, "the nature of the state is examined primarily through its size relative to that economy and the sources and structures of its income."[53] Terry Karl defines the rentier state as a state "that lives from externally generated rents rather than the surplus production of the population. In oil-exporting states, this is measured by the percentage of natural resource rents in total government revenues."[54]

Hazem Beblawi characterizes the rentier state as having four main characteristics. First, a pure rentier economy does not exist; "every economy has some elements of rent."[55] Accordingly, he defines the rentier economy as one where rent situations should predominate. The stage at which an economy becomes "rentier" is left as a matter of judgement, concurring with Mahdavy's view that determining the stage at which a state can be labelled "rentier" is arbitrary. Second, substantial rents on which the rentier economy relies should be external, that is, they must originate from foreign sources. He cites the externality of the rent origin as "crucial" because the existence of significant internal rent would indicate strong internal forces of production that could sustain the economy, thus negating the "rentier" nature of the economy. Only substantial external rent can "sustain the economy without a strong productive domestic sector, hence the epithet of a rentier economy."[56] Third, the generation of this rent or wealth must be controlled by few (usually elites), whereas the majority of the population is only involved in the distribution or consumption of it. Here, Beblawi stresses the singular importance of

---

[50] Beblawi, Hazem and Giacomo Luciani. *The Rentier State. Vol.2, Nation, State and Integration in the Arab World.* London: Croom Helm, 1987, p.11.
[51] Ibid, p.4.
[52] Ibid, p.11.
[53] Yates, Douglas. *The Rentier State in Africa*. Trenton, N.J.: Africa World Press, 1996, p. 13.
[54] Karl, Terry. "Oil-led Development: Social, Political, and Economic Consequences," in *CDDRL Working Papers.* Stanford University, 2007, p.2.
http://cddrl.stanford.edu/publications/oilled_development_social_political_and_economic_consequences/
[55] Beblawi, Hazem and Giacomo Luciani. *The Rentier State. Vol.2, Nation, State and Integration in the Arab World.* London: Croom Helm, 1987, p.51.
[56] Ibid.

this feature of the rentier economy. The fourth characteristic is closely related to the third and sees the government of a rentier state as the "principal recipient of the external rent in the economy."[57] The state, being the primary beneficiary of external rent, will consequently play a central role in distributing this wealth to the population. This lends the rentier state economic power, which can then be utilized to seize and/or consolidate political power. This concept of the rentier state is based on the assumption that such an economy leads to the creation of a "rentier mentality".

The specific characteristic that distinguishes rentier mentality from conventional economic behavior is that "it embodies a break from the work-reward causation."[58] This means that rewards in the form of income or wealth are not attained as a result of labor or performance, but instead are the result of chance or situation. Beblawi notes that most classical economists (apart from Malthus) look unfavorably upon rentiers. "Rentiers as a social group were thus assaulted by both liberal and radical economists as unproductive, almost anti-social, sharing effortlessly in the produce without, so to speak, contributing to it."[59] The distinguishing feature of the rentier is that it does not actively participate in the economic production process, but nevertheless receives a share of the profit, or rent in this case. The rentier mentality in rentier states is particularly evident in the misallocation of wealth among the general domestic population. Mahdavy notes that "whereas in most underdeveloped countries...relative regression will normally lead to public alarm and some kind of political explosion aimed at changing the status quo, in the Rentier States, the increasing welfare and prosperity (of at least part of the urban population) acquired through government expenditures and large imports pre-empts some of the urgency for change and rapid growth encountered in other countries."[60] While disparities in income and wealth may create tensions, the effects are comparatively mild relative to other developing, resource-scarce countries because rentier states are more involved in the exploitation of natural resources rather than the direct exploitation of their own citizens. This can lead to "socio-political stagnation and

---

[57] Beblawi, Hazem and Giacomo Luciani. *The Rentier State. Vol.2, Nation, State and Integration in the Arab World.* London: Croom Helm, 1987, p.52.
[58] Ibid.
[59] Ibid, p.50.
[60] Mahdavy, Hossein. "The patterns and problems of economic development in rentier states: the case of Iran." In: *M. A. Cook (ed.), Studies in the Economic History of the Middle East.* London: Oxford University Press, 1970. p. 437.

inertia,"[61] which may coincide with economic and technological underdevelopment. "The existence of relatively ample resources deludes the rentier into an expectation of ever-increasing revenues in the future," thus contributing to the inertia. Furthermore, disproportional growth in one sector of the economy may lead to an overall increase in the average economic growth rate of a rentier state. However, posting positive growth numbers can be misleading and is not always an accurate reflection of a state's long-term growth outlook. The measurement of per-capita income, for instance, includes oil profits as part of the gross national product (GNP) of rentier economies and does not illustrate the discrepancy of income distribution that exists as a result of the accumulation of rent by rentier elites and large corporations. This highlights, as demonstrated by the case of Qatar, the need and importance of analyzing alternative indicators of developmental performance instead of only purely economic indicators such as per capita income. Also, increased profits from external rents naturally tend to induce domestic spending. "Insulated by the surrounding comforts that external rent provides, rentier elites have a proclivity to form a complacent disposition and to lack the necessity that is the mother of all invention."[62] This disposition can have a profound negative effect for the productivity of rentier states.

In some Arab states, oil revenues derived from foreign purchases account for up to 90 percent of budget revenues, with only a small percentage of the labor force being engaged in the production and distribution of this oil wealth.[63] This corresponds to the definition of a rentier state and places the state or government in the important role of directing economic activity. The re-distribution of rent to the domestic population is performed through a complex form of patron-client exchanges that creates multiple layers of rent beneficiaries. In this manner, "the whole economy is arranged as a hierarchy of layers of rentiers with the state or government at the top of the pyramid, acting as the ultimate support of all other rentiers in the economy."[64] Because most rentier states impose very little to no taxes, citizens can demand far

---

[61] Mahdavy, Hossein. "The patterns and problems of economic development in rentier states: the case of Iran." In: *M. A. Cook (ed.), Studies in the Economic History of the Middle East.* London: Oxford University Press, 1970. p.437.

[62] Yates, Douglas. *The Rentier State in Africa.* Trenton, N.J.: Africa World Press, 1996, p. 21.

[63] See: Beblawi, Hazem and Giacomo Luciani. *The Rentier State. Vol.2, Nation, State and Integration in the Arab World.* London: Croom Helm, 1987, p.53.

[64] Beblawi, Hazem and Giacomo Luciani. *The Rentier State. Vol.2, Nation, State and Integration in the Arab World.* London: Croom Helm, 1987, p.53.

less in terms of political participation from their governments.[65] The contributions of external rent enables the governments of rentier states to embark on large public expenditure programs without levying taxes or running into extreme national debt or balance of payment problems that typically befalls other developing countries.[66] Oil-rich rentier states have not limited themselves only to the distribution of favors and benefits. Instead, many are providing their citizens with a broad range of public goods and services including national security, defense, health, education, welfare benefits and stable infrastructure. Moreover, the government remains the principal employer in the economy and provides relative job security coupled with lucrative salaries not available in other sectors. But, the consequences for the productive sector are severe. The state becomes the ultimate provider of private favors by doling out contracts to loyalists as an expression of gratitude. Labor efficiency wanes because of the lack of incentives and relative job security and crucial sectors of the economy like agriculture and manufacturing are neglected and abandoned in favor of more lucrative positions in the government or hydrocarbon sector. This can produce major problems for the rentier state and its economy, which will be discussed in the subsequent section.

2.3 The Rentier Economy

One of the greatest vulnerabilities of oil-dependent economies is the commodity of oil itself. There are several special attributes of oil which include: "1) its unique role as both common natural heritage of a country and the motor of global industrialization, 2) its depletability, 3) its price volatility and consequent boom-bust cycles, 4) its especially high capital-intensity and technological sophistication, 5) its enclave nature, and 6) the exceptional generation of profits that accrue to the state and to private actors."[67] Oil price changes and the global oil market have been at the center of many major political upheavals over the past few decades. The first major global oil crisis of 1973 was a direct result of the political strife between major oil-exporting Gulf states and the supporters of the Israeli Yom Kippur War.[68] By using their considerable economic leverage, the oil-exporting states (many of which were

[65] This is similar to the democratic principle of „no taxation without representation", only reversed.
[66] This is especially true for contemporary oil-exporting countries experiencing high profit-margins as a result of rising global energy prices.
[67] Karl, Terry. "Oil-led Development: Social, Political, and Economic Consequences," in *CDDRL Working Papers*. Stanford University, 2007, p.3.
http://cddrl.stanford.edu/publications/oilled_development_social_political_and_economic_consequences/
[68] The main supporters of the war included the United States, many of its allies in Western Europe, and Japan.

OPEC members) agreed to retaliate by hiking-up global oil prices and placing oil embargoes on states supporting Israel. The second oil shock of 1979 was also at the heart of a major domestic political crisis, namely the Islamic Revolution in Iran. Soaring global oil prices were the consequence of drastic reductions in Iranian oil output, which sent economic shock waves worldwide. Indeed, "the politics of oil wealth inside individual exporting countries can have great effects far from (those) domestic settings."[69] But, economic consequences in oil-importing states are not the only side-effects of oil boom and bust cycles. Whereas oil-importing states experience dramatic price increases and extensive financial losses,[70] oil-exporting states face different problems. Global oil shocks brought record profits that significantly increased the revenues available to these states. The influx of external rent caused "inflationary and Dutch disease shocks, paradoxically causing a crisis in countries that should have been enjoying the fruits of a commodity boom."[71]

Due to the volatile nature of oil, oil-dependent rentier states are highly vulnerable to external price booms and shocks. "This oil price volatility exerts a strong negative influence on budgetary discipline and the control of public finances as well as state planning, which subsequently means that economic performance deviates from planned targets by as much as 30 percent. Price volatility also exerts a negative influence on investment, income distribution and poverty alleviation."[72] The extensive inflow of external rent during boom cycles can be extremely detrimental to the rentier economy. The availability of large amounts of foreign currency leads to an increased acquisition of foreign goods due to the lack of costs of exchange. Rentier states have a tendency to facilitate the purchasing power of their currency through the maintenance of "artificially high exchange values"[73] made possible by the overabundance of foreign capital. Because the price of imported goods decreases

---

[69] Smith, Benjamin. *Hard Times in the Lands of Plenty: Oil Politics in Iran and Indonesia*. Ithaca, NY: Cornell University Press, 2007, p.2.

[70] During the oil crisis of 1973, the retail price of a gallon of gasoline in the U.S. rose from a national average of 38.5 cents to 55.1 cents within one year. The New York Stock Exchange lost shares in value of $97 billion over a period of six weeks.

[71] Smith, Benjamin. *Hard Times in the Lands of Plenty: Oil Politics in Iran and Indonesia*. Ithaca, NY: Cornell University Press, 2007, p.2

Dutch disease refers to the effect a resource boom can have on a state by causing an increase in exchange rates and a migration of labor and capital to the booming sector. This results in reduced competitiveness and higher costs of production in other sectors of its economy, which, in turn, necessitates the state to increase its imports of foreign products to compensate for the loss of domestic productivity.

[72] Karl, Terry. "Oil-led Development: Social, Political, and Economic Consequences," in *CDDRL Working Papers*. Stanford University, 2007, p.6.
http://cddrl.stanford.edu/publications/oilled_development_social_political_and_economic_consequences

[73] See: Yates, Douglas. *The Rentier State in Africa*. Trenton, N.J.: Africa World Press, 1996, p.26.

relative to the domestic currency, "imported goods have the tendency to replace domestically produced goods."[74] Foreign imports not only become cheaper, but they also have qualitative advantages over domestic products resulting from the advanced manufacturing techniques of highly industrialized states. Windfall profits also tend to raise the value of the exchange rate of currency, thus simultaneously decreasing the rate of exports from non-oil sectors of the economy such as agriculture and manufacturing.[75] Capital is reallocated to the booming oil sector in favor of the manufacturing and agricultural sectors because of the higher rate of returns. The discrepancy between the degrees of development in various sectors of rentier economies is clearly evident when the disadvantaged sectors are compared to the fairly developed sectors. The service sector, for example, experiences a relatively minimal decline because of the nature of the allocation of external rent in rentier states. "Since government is the principal recipient of oil rent, there is a tendency for bureaucracies with allocative functions to expand."[76] The expansion of the service sector at the expense of the productive sectors can achieve little economic growth, because this sector is largely unproductive and "cannot replicate the productive structure of a modern industrial society nor even a traditional agricultural one."[77]

Embarking on costly development projects is also not the answer to the effective promotion of economic development. Petroleum production is one of the world's most cost-intensive industries, requiring modern, foreign technology. "Rather than enlarging the goods-producing capacity of the economy, inter-sectoral linkages tend to be negligible because of the high import intensity of infrastructural construction activities."[78] In short, since productive linkages to other sectors of the economy tend to be weak, they promote weak job growth in terms of the broader economy. The capital intensive nature of the petroleum industry creates little employment because most of the jobs in this sector require skills that are not readily available in the profile of the domestic populace in rentier states. Additionally, the creation of wealth without effort undermines the concept of work ethics and breeds a negative perception of certain types of labor, especially manual labor. The sudden inflow of oil-wealth causes domestic workers to become accustomed to receiving relatively high salaries for comparably little work. Also, domestic workers do not

---

[74] Yates, Douglas. *The Rentier State in Africa*. Trenton, N.J.: Africa World Press, 1996, p.24.
[75] This is referred to as Dutch disease.
[76] Yates, Douglas. *The Rentier State in Africa*. Trenton, N.J.: Africa World Press, 1996, p.26.
[77] Ibid., p.29.
[78] Ibid., p.25.

"have much to gain from the risks and pains of active work when they get easier benefits from rent sharing through sponsoring, import trade, brokerage or real estate and housing speculation."[79] This prompts rentier states to "import" foreign employees who possess more disciplined work and fiscal habits to perform the labor local citizens are unwilling to do. The influx of migrant workers, in turn, results in increased foreign remittances contributing to the outflow of capital.

Increased government spending can also facilitate corruption in rentier states. Most expenditure programs in rentier states are under the direct control of the government, high-ranking officials, their subordinates and family members. Michael Field observes that "if a prince heads to a ministry or some other government department, it is accepted that he is entitled to draw on the budget of that department or take a share of its spending in major projects."[80] There is little distinction between public and private interests due to the extreme concentration of political and economic power. Holding public office provides officials with the opportunity to pursue rent-seeking activities in order to further personal interests and wealth. High levels of corruption ensue because of weak state capacity and institutional restraint. The case of Saudi Arabian military expenditures in the 1980's highlights the high levels of corruption that are rampant in rentier states. During the 1980's, Saudi Arabia's outlays on national security were among the highest in the world and by 1989, its expenditures of $14.7 billion ranked eleventh among the countries of the world. Before the onset of the Gulf War in 1990, those numbers rose to $31.9 billion to meet U.S. and British military costs, with Saudi Arabia being the chief financial contributor. Even with significant military expenditures stretching over decades, Saudi Arabia by 1990 did not have the individual capacity to protect its own borders nor aid neighboring Kuwait from the Iraqi invasion, necessitating the involvement and financial support of foreign American and British troops. Most of the modern military equipments that were purchased from Western allies such as the U.S., Britain, and France could barely be operated by the Saudis. They were either placed in storage or were operated by foreign mercenaries.[81] Ultimately, these arms deals were mostly

[79]Beblawi, Hazem and Giacomo Luciani, eds. *The Rentier State.* London, New York, Sydney: Croom Helm, 1987, p.111.
[80] Field, Michael. *The Merchants: Big Business Families of Arabia.* London: John Murray Publishers, 1984, pp. 101-102.
[81] Margolis, Eric. "The Mother of all Scandals." June 19, 2007. http://www.lewrockwell.com/margolis/margolis79.html

about buying military protection from western states instead of an earnest effort to truly modernize and develop the Saudi Arabian military.

High levels of corruption and productive inefficiency hinder one of the most important alternatives rentier economies have to oil-dependency, namely diversification, and this leads to what is known as a rentier mentality. Because the rentier state has the capacity to support itself with external rents, there has been little need for it to impose unpopular taxes on citizens or develop its extractive capacities for the purposes of tax collection. This can be advantageous for rentiers over the short-term because windfall profits enable them to "purchase" the consent of the governed without resorting to taxation. "Because it spends and does not tax, the rentier class is liberated from the reliance on legitimation by its society and thus suffers no serious challenge to its power."[82] Over the long-term, however, exposure to extreme fluctuations of price can cause internal turmoil and instability because it directly affects the administrative, structural, and spending capacities of rentier states. Consequently, they are forced to limit government expenditures, which may lend increased importance to socio-political factors. But, limiting government expenditure has not drastically altered the primary structure and source of government revenues in oil-dependent states.[83] Because most rentier states have not developed efficient administrative and extractive capacities for the purposes of taxation, they may suffer from "inefficiency in any field of activity that requires extensive organizational inputs."[84] Whereas during oil booms, rentier states have the capability to coerce and bribe dissidents and political pressure groups, the decrease of external rents during oil shocks leaves them highly susceptible to such threats. This may result in long-term political repercussions and instability.

A robust tax system has several important functions that are essential for the state. First, taxation can have a monitoring function by providing valuable information about citizens and society, effectively serving as an information-gathering mechanism for the government. Taxing various social groups also requires the government to make concessions to its citizens (similar to the revolutionary American maxim of "no

[82] Yates, Douglas. *The Rentier State in Africa*. Trenton, N.J.: Africa World Press, 1996, p.35.
[83] For a detailed account, see: Yates, Douglas. *The Rentier State in Africa*. Trenton, N.J.: Africa World Press, 1996, p.23.
[84] Mahdavy, Hossein. "The patterns and problems of economic development in rentier states: the case of Iran." In: *M. A. Cook (ed.), Studies in the Economic History of the Middle East*. London: Oxford University Press, 1970. p.467.

taxation without representation") in exchange for non-oil based revenue. This creates social interaction between government and society and lends the state legitimacy while allowing it to monitor potential social/political dissidents or groups. Second, a gradual tax-extraction process that presents state bureaucracies with the time to expand and develop while providing citizens the opportunity to acclimatize to taxation is important for long-term stability. Benjamin Smith notes that the sudden imposition of taxes during bust cycles, for instance, may provoke violent resistance from political dissidents and social groups.[85] Finally, the development of a stable and efficient tax bureaucracy can further serve to strengthen the overall institutional capacity of the state.

2.4 The Rentier Mentality

The lack of an effective tax-collecting administration in rentier states leads to a widespread rentier mentality and can be attributed to several factors. Because the productive sectors tend to be underdeveloped or neglected in rentier economies, there is very little the government can actually tax. Also, in light of significant profits accrued from oil exports during boom cycles, taxation is deemed to be "unnecessary". As long as the state, "whose power is magnified by the autonomy of (its) source of revenue,"[86] focuses on the allocation and distribution of wealth instead of tax collection, society cannot make any demands on it. Also, public expenditure is the driving force of the rentier economy; external rent comprises the largest percentage of GDP, thus domestic spending can only contribute to GDP growth. The absence of taxation combined with generous public expenditure programs conveys a sense of generosity to the individual citizen towards the rentier state. Thus, instead of accusing the state for the uneven distribution of benefits and wealth, individuals seek to further their personal interests by cooperating with the government. A lack of political and civil leverage and the citizen's minimal economic contribution to the state diffuses the objective grounds on which he can demand an increase in benefits. "Class based politics are impossible because the economic conditions and sectoral imbalances of the rentier state discourage class formation."[87] That is, the unequal development of various sectors of the economy provides little opportunity for social mobilization. Not all segments of society or the economy suffer under the rentier

[85] Smith, Benjamin. *Hard Times in the Lands of Plenty: Oil Politics in Iran and Indonesia.* Ithaca, NY: Cornell University Press, 2007, p.52.
[86] Yates, Douglas. *The Rentier State in Africa.* Trenton, N.J.: Africa World Press, 1996, p.34.
[87] Ibid.

system, thus the sectors that are enjoying the fruits of external rent profits act as a counterbalance to other, less prosperous sectors. In addition, actors in society attempt to curry the favor of the elite and acquire key positions and parts of the state bureaucracy. This type of behavior is regarded as legitimate since "popularity rather than performance determines the position of the elite."[88] Furthermore, the loyalty of citizens is "to the system, not to individuals in power."[89] As long as the rentier system functions, there is seldom any true political debate. This is also because of the vast number of individuals and social groups who have their interests vested in those of the state. Only a reduction in external rent or its misallocation can induce substantial political or social dissent domestically. Luciani maintains that the "inequality of distribution is not an issue, but if the search for personal advantage leads to a failure in cashing in fully the potential rent,"[90] the issue of corruption becomes important. Rentier states have little interest in democracy and democratic principles. The establishment of representative bodies in rentier states acts more as a mechanism to vent and control popular discontent instead of providing citizens with a venue to voice social and political views on the national stage. Also, since the economic interests of citizens not belonging to the rentier elite is disregarded, principally parties that represent only cultural or ideological orientation or state-inspired parties are formed. Because rents permit the government to "buy" legitimacy, regime stability is heavily dependent on foreign revenues in rentier states. That is why the preservation of the status quo has utmost priority. As long as the state maintains its popularity through public allocation and distribution programs without resorting to public taxation, there is a decreased likelihood of threats to its "security and elite status within the power structure premised on the inflow of external rents."[91] Terry Karl notes that with "basic needs met by an often generous welfare state, with the absence of taxation, and with little more than demands for quiescence and loyalty in return, populations tend to be politically inactive, relatively obedient and loyal and levels of protest remain low -- at least as long as the oil state can deliver. Thus for long periods an unusual

[88] Yates, Douglas. *The Rentier State in Africa*. Trenton, N.J.: Africa World Press, 1996, p.34.
[89] Beblawi, Hazem and Giacomo Luciani, eds. *The Rentier State*. London, New York, Sydney: Croom Helm, 1987, p.75.
[90] Ibid.
[91] Yates, Douglas. *The Rentier State in Africa*. Trenton, N.J.: Africa World Press, 1996, p.36.

combination of dependence, passivity, and entitlement marks the political culture of petroleum exporters."[92]

Different theoretical arguments of the rentier theory illustrate both the strengths and limitations of external rent dependent states. The following section examines the main arguments by which external rent both instigates political and social crises and serves as a mechanism to boost regime resilience.

Karl argues that while state expenditures promote cooptation, they help to support repression and expand repressive apparatuses. Rentier states tend to spend more money on military expenditures than their non-resource dependent counterparts. The significant amount of wealth invested demonstrates the close association between extensive oil revenues and the development and modernization of the military sector. A strong military in rentier states serves the purpose of reinforcing and supporting the ruling regime while reducing political and popular dissent through coercion and cooptation. Based on this assumption, oil wealth is "a positive predictor of greater regime durability."[93] What is more, oil-importing states have a vested interest in the continued stability of oil-exporters, making rentier states less susceptible to exogenous pressures and to make calls for democratization or the advancement of human rights. This increases the likelihood of the use of repression in rentier states due to the lack of consequences or sanctions. A visit by President G. W. Bush to the Middle East in January of 2008 revealed plans to sell the Saudi government approximately $120 million in sophisticated bombs as well as offering the five other military packages to the United Arab Emirates and Kuwait, bringing the total value to about $11.5 billion.[94] These military packages are part of a U.S. strategy to further bolster the defenses of allied, oil-producing Gulf nations, although the Saudi government is considered to be one of the most repressive regimes in the world. The unconstrained use of repression combined with external oil profits help rentier states to consolidate power and endure over longer periods of time, providing there remains a consistent inflow of rent. Boom periods confer the state the capability to buy-off potential opponents and can prolong the state's existence. Others argue that oil-dependency and rent-seeking can undermine political stability, especially

---

[92] Karl, Terry. "Oil-led Development: Social, Political, and Economic Consequences," in *CDDRL Working Papers*. Stanford University, 2007, p.21.
http://cddrl.stanford.edu/publications/oilled_development_social_political_and_economic_consequences/
[93] Ibid., p.23.
[94] Fox News. "Bush Visits Saudi Arabia for Talks With King Abdullah." January, 2008.
http://www.foxnews.com/story/0,2933,322467,00.html

during bust cycles. Due to the lack of an extractive fiscal policy, rentier states maintain a high degree of autonomy from society. This can result in "weak state-society linkages and ought to produce subsequent instability both during booms, when politicians are likely to flood the domestic economy with revenues, spending unwisely and spurring destabilizing inflation, and busts, when weak state institutions prove unable to continue patronage and external revenues from domestic sources."[95] The source of legitimacy in rentier states is external rent, which acts as the main "glue of polity."[96] Once this consolidating factor is dissolved, rentier states are more likely to collapse during periods of bust than non-resource dependent states which have established a stable foundation based on strong institutional organs, administrative capacities, and developed legitimate mechanisms of social control. But, even during boom periods, rentier states are vulnerable to destabilizing factors such as Dutch Disease, which can damage the viability of key non-oil sectors by increasing the currency's value and discouraging production and export in the agricultural and manufacturing sectors.[97]

[95] Smith, Benjamin. *Hard Times in the Lands of Plenty: Oil Politics in Iran and Indonesia.* Ithaca, NY: Cornell University Press, 2007, p.18.

[96] See: Karl, Terry. "Oil-led Development: Social, Political, and Economic Consequences," in *CDDRL Working Papers.* Stanford University, 2007, p.24. http://cddrl.stanford.edu/publications/oilled_development_social_political_and_economic_consequences/

[97] See: Smith, Benjamin. *Hard Times in the Lands of Plenty: Oil Politics in Iran and Indonesia.* Ithaca, NY: Cornell University Press, 2007, p.19.

3. POST-REVOLUTIONARY IRAN: ECONOMIC AND POLITICAL DEVELOPMENTS

The following chapters trace politico-economic developments in the IRI after 1979. They provide a brief historical account of the preceding economic developments leading up to the Islamic Revolution and a detailed evaluation of political and economic developments after 1979. The post-revolutionary period will be divided into four phases. The first phase analyzes the Islamic faction's seizure of power under the leadership of Ayatollah Khomeini, their conservative economic policy and consolidation of state authority, the subsequent Iran-Iraq war, and the rise of Islamic-populism. The second phase experiences a shift of political power in favor of moderate candidates; it focuses on the abandonment of the populist and closed-door policies of the preceding decade with the aim of boosting economic growth and development while attaining a certain degree of self-sufficiency. The IRI's pursuit of liberalization reforms and its impact on political and economic development will be discussed in detail. The third phase focuses on the reformist President Mohammad Khatami and his introduction of socio-economic liberalization reforms. The final phase will briefly analyse the return of the conservatives to power, the rise of President Mahmoud Ahmadinejad, and the return to traditionalist political and economic policies. Various economic sectors, their performance and the expanding active role of the state will be analyzed in order to determine what factor or factors have contributed to state resilience in the IRI over a period of thirty years.

3.1 Socio-Economic Developments in Pre-Revolutionary Iran

The two decades preceding the Islamic Revolution of 1979 demonstrated a period of impressive economic and social development in Iran. Comprehensive socio-economic reforms undertaken by Shah Mohammad Reza Pahlavi transformed a primarily agrarian and stagnant economy into a modern, progressive economy characterized by rapid urbanization and industrialization. Windfall oil profits in the 1960's and 1970's resulted in increased public expenditures and contributed to the growing role of the state and the public sector. Also, these revenues provided the Pahlavi regime with the capacity to initiate a series of socio-economic programs with the intent to bring about systematic changes including the expansion of the private sector, improved social welfare, the sale of state enterprises to the public, extension of women's rights, land reform, the nationalization of forests/pasturelands, and the establishment of a Literacy and Health Corps. Termed as the "White Revolution", this multibillion dollar public investment project was fuelled by soaring oil revenues and allowed the Iranian state to circumvent state expenditure restrictions and heavy foreign loans. According to World Bank estimates, Iran averaged an annual real growth rate of 9.6% during 1960-1977, higher than any other nation. Over the same time span, the agricultural sector grew nearly 5%, the industrial sector by 8.7%, and the service sector by an average of 13%. The oil and gas sector experienced the largest average annual growth rate of 14.5% during 1960 to 1974. Oil exports rose from approximately 1 million barrels per day (mb/d) in 1963 to a peak of nearly 6 mb/d in 1974, induced by the sharp rise in global oil prices resulting from the OPEC embargo. This was achieved by the overexploitation of oil wells and boosted the state's oil revenues in 1974/75 to almost 18 billion; compared to the previous years' profit margin of $4.6 billion, this represented an almost fourfold increase.

However, the rapid modernization agenda of the Shah was flawed and did not incorporate various social classes and groups into its program. The state did not need to integrate, cooperate or make concessions to the general public in order to implement its modernization policies because it enjoyed relative financial autonomy made possible by external oil revenues. Social groups such as the Iranian *bazaaris*, along with the clergy, the working class and the poor were marginalized, persecuted, or ignored.[98] His exclusion of these important groups would come back to haunt him in the following years. For instance, the *bazaar*, at that time, "constituted a series of cooperative hierarchies (long-term, multifaceted, and cross-cutting ties) fostering a great sense of group solidarity despite differences in economic power, social status and, political proclivities."[99] This social faction demonstrated a great capacity to mobilize large masses and possessed extensive financial and social resources. Despite attempts by the Shah to curb the *bazaar's* power and influence in the 1960's and 1970's, he failed to dismantle its economic institutions and autonomy. Instead, his efforts further "fostered the Bazaar's autonomy and a concentration of commercial value chains within the physical confines of the marketplace."[100] By 1979, the

---

[98] The term "*bazaari*" refers to members of the Iranian *bazaar*, or marketplace, which constitutes an important socio-economic faction that played a significant role in the overthrow of the Pahlavi monarchy in 1979. For a detailed account of the Iranian *bazaar*, see: Keshavarzian, Arang. *Bazaar and State in Iran.* Cambridge: Cambridge University Press, 2007.

[99] Keshavarzian, Arang. *Bazaar and State in Iran.* Cambridge: Cambridge University Press, 2007, p.3.

[100] Ibid., p.3.

bazaaris had joined the growing coalition of opposition groups against the Pahlavi state and played a key role in its overthrow.

Ultimately, social and economic woes exacerbated the growing instability of the Shah's state. In light of the windfall oil profits, the next two years witnessed a drastic increase in public expenditures which caused high inflation rates and a deepening gap between aggregate supply and demand. The high rise in demand could not be met by domestic production, causing economic imbalances, supply shortages and spurring an increase in the import of foreign goods. Decreased global demand for oil in 1977 coupled with a higher expenditure to oil profit ratio brought an end to the Iranian economic boom. The unexpected decline in oil revenues forced the Pahlavi government to take international loans to meet domestic spending needs amidst gross budget deficits and low global oil prices. Deflationary policies were adopted by the state to curb soaring prices, cut public expenditure, and reduce credits. But, these measures were introduced a little too late amidst rising unemployment and a series of political disturbances that led to three changes in the government. By 1978, oil output had declined to 5.3 mb/d, with 4.5 mb/d being sold abroad. Drastic boom and bust cycles caused by the volatility of global oil prices created favorable conditions for socio-political dissent. The uprising of an alliance of anti-Shah groups and the indefinite strike of the Tudeh-influenced oil workers in October 1978 further instigated a dramatic decrease in state revenues and ultimately culminated in the overthrow of the Pahlavi regime and the establishment of an Islamic republic under the leadership of Grand Ayatollah Ruhollah Khomeini.

The oil-dependent economic structure of Iran under the Pahlavi government demonstrated moderate capabilities when faced with economic challenges. It managed to weather times of significant economic hardships, but it was not able to survive the onslaught of antagonistic social and political forces that had mobilized against the state. The overambitious socio-economic projects undertaken by Mohammad Reza Shah in an attempt to catapult the country to the position of a major industrial power within a short period of time based principally on a highly unreliable source of revenue, namely oil, proved to be too burdensome.

4. PHASE I: 1979-1988, ISLAMIC POPULISM AND THE CONSOLIDATION OF POWER

The period after the toppling of the Pahlavi dynasty in 1979 proved to be tumultuous for the IRI in both political and economic terms. The overriding popularity of the revolutionary movement managed to mobilize a broad spectrum of various social classes (i.e. urban poor, public servants, working class, *bazaaris*, intellectuals, bourgeoisie, etc.) in Iran towards attaining a single, principal goal, namely to end the regime of the Shah and to establish social justice and equality. Diverse revolutionary forces that had managed to oust the Shah from power did not have specific political and economic agendas that were acceptable to all rival factions; the disparate coalition of groups that succeeded in overthrowing the Shah quickly dismantled. A number of divergent interests, all vying for power, were represented by the various factions: Khomeini's loyalists and their militant clergymen allies envisioned a form of government based wholly on Islamic principles and under the guidance of orthodox clerics; Leftists and Marxists, represented by the *Tudeh* and *Fedai Khalq* organizations, wanted the current revolution to evolve into a Socialist Revolution; additional radical Islamic leftists such as the *Mujahedin-e Khalq Organization* (MKO) wanted to create a classless Islamic society by combining both Marxist-Leninist and Shia Islam principles; liberal secularists like the National Front group, on the other hand, favored a more social democratic approach; *bazaaris* wanted greater economic involvement; Islamic progressives, represented by the Liberation Movement of Iran and led by Mehdi Bazargan proposed a more moderate, "Euro-socialist system" suffused with Islamic undertones.[101] A national referendum was held on March 30 and 31 to determine the kind of political system to be established. The only option to appear on the ballot was a government that combined "Republican" and "Islamic" structures into a single state system. Khomeini rejected the demands of various opposition groups and one of his chief rivals, Ayatollah Shariatmadari, to add alternative choices.[102] Due to the extensive networks based in mosques throughout the country and the consolidation of control over society through so-called Revolutionary *Komitehs* and the creation of his own Islamic Republican Party (IRP),

[101] See: Amuzegar, Jahangir. *Iran's Economy Under the Islamic Republic*, New York and London: I. B. Tauris, 1993, p.17.
[102] At the time, Ayatollah Shariatmadari was among the highest-ranking Shia clerics in Iran who played a key role in the revolution of 1979. Known for his somewhat liberal views, he led one of the political factions against Khomeini and founded the Islamic People's Republican Party in 1979.

Khomeini's supporters claimed victory over other anti-Shah groups.[103] The state reported a turnout of 89% with 98% of the voters overwhelmingly in favor of an Islamic republic. On April 1, 1979, Khomeini proclaimed the official establishment of the Islamic Republic of Iran. The Constitution, drafted in 1979, was based on the *velayat-e faqih* (Rule of the Jurisprudent) and described Ayatollah Ruhollah Khomeini as a *marja-e taqlid* (Source of Emulation) and the Leader of the Islamic Republic.[104] But, "given the hierarchy of jurisprudential *ejtehad* (authority) in Shi'ism, and that the Islamic republic failed to incorporate this hierarchy fully in the formal structure of the state, a dual structure of authority developed in post-revolutionary Iran."[105] Thus, factional conflicts could not be easily resolved through formal state structures and domestic political stability could not be fully established. Also, the lack of viable social and legal institutions prolonged the post-revolutionary economic reconstruction process.

A bomb attack, detonated by the MKO in 1981, killed over fifty of the highest-ranking officials of Khomeini's government (including his second-highest ranking official at the time, Chief Justice Mohammad Beheshti). With the prospect of a continuing and widespread civil war looming on the horizon, the state decided to pursue a strategy of cooptation and coercion. It realized that viable stability could best be achieved through cooperation under circumstances of economic hardships, a war with Iraq, and declining oil profits. Because Khomeini's government initially lacked the financial resources to buy the loyalty of opposition groups and potential coalition partners, it was forced to make major concessions by handing over control of newly seized properties and economic assets to various social factions. The *bazaaris*, for instance, received such assets "in the form of directorships of newly established religious foundations."[106] Ironically, the *bazaar* had enjoyed a great degree of autonomy, economic influence and considerable mobilizational capacity under the Pahlavi regime, which actually sought to diminish and isolate its power. Khomeini, on the other hand, stressed the importance of the *bazaar* for the state and

---

[103] After having served the purpose of establishing clerical authority and rule in the IRI, the Islamic Republican Party was dissolved in 1987.
[104] Hiro, Dilip. *Iran Today*. London: Politico's Publishing, 2006, p. 133.
[105] Rahnema, Saeed and Sohrab Behdad (eds.) *Iran After The Revolution: Crisis Of An Islamic State.* London and New York: I.B. Taurius, 1995, p.99.
[106] Smith, Benjamin. *Hard Times in the Lands of Plenty: Oil Politics in Iran and Indonesia.* Ithaca, NY: Cornell University Press, 2007, p.164.
The role of these religious foundations, or *bonyads*, will be discussed in a subsequent section.
Benjamin Smith notes that these concessions marked the end of a period of conflict between Khomeini's regime and the *bazaar*.

vice versa and declared his will to collaborate with its members; however, close interaction and cooptation with the *bazaar* allowed the state to monitor it more closely and enhanced the government's ability to exercise greater social control. Under the Islamic republic, the *bazaar* was transformed into a "coercive hierarchy" with a diminished sense of collective solidarity that has limited its capacity to mobilize against the state.[107] Thus, through coercive measures and cooperation, Khomeini was able to accomplish that which the Shah could not achieve through isolation and force, namely the fragmentation and weakening of the *bazaar's* ability to mobilize against the state.

As aforementioned, initially, the IRI did not have immediate access to substantial amounts of oil rents directly after the revolution in 1979 to "pay-off" political rivals and opposition groups. Instead, it was forced to make concessions and compromises, co-opt with rival factions, and build alliances with other social and political groups. After this difficult initiation period, the state sought to expand its authoritative and administrative capacity by strengthening state institutions to reinforce its position and attain greater social control. The widespread support among the broader population for the integration of Islamic principles into state structures provided the state with the necessary legitimacy to establish formal, religious state institutions that run parallel to representative institutions under a single constitutional framework. For example, while there is an elected president as the head of the executive branch, the Supreme Leader, appointed by the Assembly of Experts, acts as the head of state; similarly, regular courts are matched by revolutionary courts; the army (*Artesh*) by the Iranian Revolutionary Guards (*Sepah*); there is an elected parliament (*Majlis*) but also an appointed Guardian Council, which serves as the upper house of parliament.[108] There are five principal centers of power, consisting of:

1. the Supreme Leader (or *rahbar*), who is both the spiritual, military and secular head of the state and holds the most powerful position in the IRI;
2. the Assembly of Experts, which elects the Supreme Leader and monitors his performance;

---

[107] Keshavarzian characterizes a „coercive hierarchy" as „short-term, single-faceted, and fragmented relations" within the *bazaar*. For a detailed account, see:
Keshavarzian, Arang. *Bazaar and State in Iran.* Cambridge: Cambridge University Press, 2007, p.3.

[108] See: Atieh Bahar. *Iran Country Profile and Business Guide Geography, Population, & Climate Change, 2002.*
www.atiehbahaar.com

3. the president, who acts as the chief executive (however, he does not possess control of the country's armed forces; this right is reserved for the Supreme Leader);
4. the Parliament (*Majlis*)
5. and the judiciary.

Two additional institutions, namely the Guardian Council and the Expediency Council, are also important components of the IRI's state infrastructure. The former ensures the compatibility of legislation with Islamic law and the Constitution and while the latter acts as a moderator between the President the *Majlis*, and the Guardian Council. Although formally, the IRI's political state structure was designed to make each political and institutional body accountable both vertically and horizontally through a system of checks and balances, this is not the case in practice. The religious, unelected state institutions and leaders like the Expediency Council, the Supreme Leader, and the Head of Judiciary enjoy a high degree of autonomy and very little accountability. This is because the structure of power in Iran is comprised of many inter-connected and autonomous rings headed by individuals who are more important than the position they occupy.[109] Thus, hypothetically, if an influential individual changes his post, he can transfer his power from the old position to the new. The most powerful individuals in the state are traditionalist clergymen chiefly occupying positions in the influential, unelected and religious institutions of the state. Their capacity to trump any major political decisions originating from elected institutions provides the conservative clergy with great leeway to impose their political will, both on rival factions in the state and on society in general. With the power to ban any candidates deemed as "un-Islamic" or unfit to run for public office, members of the unelected branch of the state can directly influence the political course of the country. Moreover, they can extend their influence to other segments of the state because most important positions are rewarded by them to their own close relatives, friends, or loyalists. Thus, indicative of a rentier mentality, personal and patrimonial modes of patronage are the rule when it comes to the distribution of key government posts and the promotion of civil servants within the hierarchy of the state.[110]

---

[109] See: Amirahmadi, Hooshang. *Iran's Power Structure*, March, 18, 1996. http://www.iranian.com/Mar96/Opinion/AmirIran.html
[110] Ibid.

Figure 2: The Structure of Power in the Islamic Republic of Iran

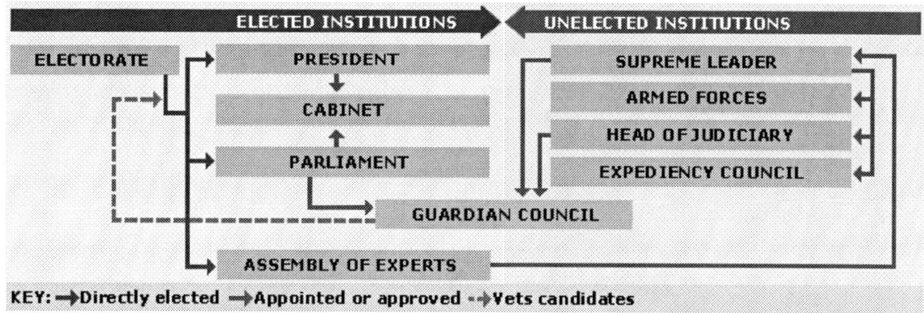

Source: BBC News. "In Depth: Iran, Who Holds the Power?" 2008
http://news.bbc.co.uk/2/shared/spl/hi/middle_east/03/iran_power/html/default.stm

An extensive institution-building process also followed on a smaller scale which increased the power and influence of local governments and set up religious foundations to strengthen state-society relations and keep an eye on potential dissidents and/or opponents. Through these apparatuses, the government strived to extend central control by increasing society's reliance on state funding, subsidies, investment projects and general public expenditures. Thus, the loyalty of public servants serving in local governments or those dependent on financial support from *bonyads* was "purchased" by offers of higher wages, social welfare funds, capital grants and scholarships, job security and payoffs. This method of political patronage, a key attribute of a rentier states, enhanced interdependency within state institutions, reinforced state-society relations, and enabled the conservative, authoritarian government to hold onto effective political control.

With Khomeini and his allies in power, all secular socio-economic agendas were dispelled and the state set out to establish an Islamic society and economy. "At issue were the questions of the nation's economic *orientation,* the shape of its basic economic *institutions*, and the *direction* of economic policies."[111] The western development model of the Pahlavi regime was heavily criticized for the over-exploitation of the country's oil supplies, underdevelopment and neglect of various sectors of the economy (i.e. agriculture), and the heavy dependence on foreign

[111] Amuzegar, Jahangir. *Iran's Economy Under the Islamic Republic*, New York and London: I. B. Tauris, 1993, p.16.

imports and trade. In addition, the Shah's economic stance was said to have widened the gap between the rich and poor, marginalized traditional cultural groups, and failed to benefit the majority of the populace. The Shah, at the time of the revolution, was considered by a majority of Iranians as a pawn of the United States which indirectly sought to impose its influence and dominance on Iran through him. "The revolution of 1979 was perceived as a direct cultural and nationalistic reaction to Western imperialism; and it represented a strong will to rebuild the society after an ideal homegrown model."[112] This direct reaction to exogenous pressures, either real or perceived, is an attribute of the IRI that has served as an effective mechanism for the current government in Tehran to rally the domestic populace to its cause against a common enemy.

Fundamental principles of the Islamic economy (as defined by the new government) were incorporated in the Constitution and its basic tenets and objectives were communicated to the public by the leaders of the Islamic Republic in their Friday prayer meetings. Islamic economics in Iran "refers to a set of socio-economic principles concerning production, consumption, and distribution that are designed to create a "just society", and certain individual attitudes and behavior that are likely to ensure a society of "divine unity"."[113] Under an ideal Islamic economy, the state takes a more active and direct role in the economy in order to ensure, for instance, the equal and "equitable" distribution of income and wealth. It also seeks to establish a certain degree of homogeneity and moderation in society (that is, the Islamic state is opposed to waste, lavishness, and extravagance), promote industrial independence from foreign powers by limiting the imports of foreign goods, and restructure internal consumption patterns.[114] Thus, the chief official economic policy of Khomeini's newly established government was to "re-orient Iranian society toward Islamic social justice, and to restructure the Iranian economy to attain self-reliance and self-sufficiency."[115]

4.1 The Islamist-Populist, Socio-Economic Agenda

The years 1978-82 and 1986-89 were characterized by an economic recession and an economic slowdown, respectively, whereas 1982-86 marked a

[112] Amuzegar, Jahangir. *Iran's Economy Under the Islamic Republic*, New York and London: I. B. Tauris, 1993, p.16.
[113] Ibid., p.19.
[114] Ibid., p.22.
[115] Ibid., p.23.

period of recovery and growth.[116] Several internal and external factors can be attributed to the fluctuations in Iran's GDP output during the decade following the Islamic Revolution. Internal factors include the outsourcing of vast amounts of capital, the emigration of numerous professionals and skilled workers, post-revolutionary political and social unrest, increased corruption facilitated by the acquisition of large businesses by the government and its sympathizers and contradictions and ambiguities regarding labor laws and property rights under the new framework of an Islamic establishment. External factors such as the eight-year war with neighboring Iraq, sinking global oil prices, the imposition of international economic sanctions due to Iran's refusal to abide by United Nations (UN) resolutions, the influx of foreign refugees from Iraq and Afghanistan and the freezing of Iranian foreign exchange assets all placed significant strains on the IRI's economy.[117]

Comprehensive economic restructuring after the revolutionary turmoil was one of the top priorities of the newly established Provisional Revolutionary Government in the summer of 1979. Due the void left by the mass exodus of owners and workers from their corporations, the new state began a series of confiscations and takeovers. It pushed for the nationalization of major economic sectors and brought under the state's possession banks, insurance companies and numerous industrial and manufacturing corporations. Furthermore, foreign trade and the oil sector were nationalized; the banking system was revamped to create interest-free banking; and the government's allocative, distributional, and regulatory role in the economy were expanded. Thus, the confiscation of properties and billions of dollars in assets of the former upper class and royal family, from banks, and homeowners in pre-revolutionary Iran were transferred to "public" ownership. Most of these assets were utilized to form a new type of institution in the form of charitable foundations, or *bonyads*. These parastatal foundations are under the control of the Supreme Leader, operate hundreds of companies, are mostly exempt from taxation and are involved in activities ranging from commerce to social services. In addition, they play a significant role in functioning as a key proxy for the exercise of power, the redistribution of resources and a bridge between state structures and socio-economic developments. "They also serve as mechanisms for untaxed savings and investment,

---

[116] See: Amuzegar, Jahangir. *Iran's Economy Under the Islamic Republic*, New York and London: I. B. Tauris, 1993, p.43.
[117] Ibid.

as well as providing for the financial independence of the religious hierarchy from the auspices of the state."[118] Because of their control of vast amounts of financial resources and their proximity to various social groups (i.e. traditional merchants, or bazaaris), *bonyads* serve to further consolidate power and exert social control, especially in venues where conventional state authority cannot usually be exercised.

For instance, one of the most notable charitable foundations, the *Bonyad-e Shahid* (Martyr's Foundation), has accrued funds from government subsidies and property expropriations totalling 398.5 billion rials.[119] Its influence is wide-ranging and includes the ownership of numerous private enterprises active in sectors as diverse as agriculture, industry, commerce and production. In addition, it "oversees the distribution of special rights to its constituency, including prioritized university admission and employment consideration, as well as other benefits including assistance with arranging marriages."[120] The most prominent and influential charitable foundation is the *Bonyad-e Mostazafan* (Foundation for the Oppressed). It reportedly controls "$12 billion in assets, including an estimated 400,000 workers in thousands of enterprises and properties ranging from agriculture, trade and industry, housing development and construction, transportation (land, shipping, and aviation) and tourism."[121] These powerful *bonyads*, among others, allow the religious theocracy in the IRI to wield and exert power and influence outside of the institutional framework of the state. They are subject to virtually no government oversight and are "an accurate reflection of the bifurcated nature of authority" in Iran.[122]

The nationalization of the National Iranian Oil Company (NIOC) signified another major step towards the expansion of state capacity and power. Bloomberg and Ahram note that the 1979 Islamic constitution officially enshrined the concept of public ownership and state administration of oil under state control, specifying that mineral wealth "be at the disposal of the Islamic government for it to utilize in accordance with the public interest."[123] Its nationalization was initially intended to

---

[118] Alizadeh, Parvin. *"The Economy of Iran: Dilemmas of an Islamic State."* London and New York, I.B. Tauris, 2000, p.149.

[119]Ibid., p.151.
Note: Available data providing detailed financial data about the Iranian *bonyads* is limited due to their closed accounts.

[120] Alizadeh, Parvin. *"The Economy of Iran: Dilemmas of an Islamic State."* London and New York, I.B. Tauris, 2000, p.151.

[121]Alizadeh, Parvin. *"The Economy of Iran: Dilemmas of an Islamic State."* London and New York, I.B. Tauris, 2000, p.153.

[122] Ibid., p.150.

[123] Brumberg, Daniel and Ariel Ahram. *The National Iranian Oil Company in Iranian Politics.* The James A. Baker III Institute for Public Policy, Rice University, 2007, p.7.

ensure the reduction of foreign involvement in the Iranian oil industry, curtail the overproduction and overexploitation of oil fields and assure the just distribution of oil rents to the general public. The integration of inexperienced Islamic clerics and theocrats into the NIOC infrastructure proved to be detrimental to the attainment of these goals. Difficulties caused by the Iran-Iraq war, the withdrawal of Western investment and the reduction of Iranian oil output facilitated a period of economic challenges for the IRI and the NIOC. During the 1980's, the NIOC pursued a series of opaque policies in an effort to circumvent international arms embargoes and to compensate for the decline in oil revenues. It participated in covert negotiations and arms deals with third parties and Western corporations to acquire additional supplies for its eight-year war with Iraq. In order to boost oil revenues, the NIOC expanded its customer base to include Japanese, Pakistani, Turkish and Soviet bloc firms.[124] Moreover, the diversification of oil exports to new customers was intended to reduce the IRI's susceptibility to Western boycotts and to steer away from traditional customers that had dealings with the deposed Shah's preceding government. Such actions compromised the NIOC's professionalism and ultimately "left a debilitating legacy by associating NIOC with patterns of rent-seeking and corruption" in the following years.[125] Following its nationalization, the NIOC has essentially been transformed into a multi-functional instrument of the state's expanded administrative capacity in a number of ways. First, the complete control of the country's hydrocarbon resources through the NIOC provides the government with the financial liberty and flexibility to embark on expenditure programs without having to concede to public demand. Second, the NIOC's access to a vast network of economic and political venues is an efficient mechanism for the redistribution of oil rents to key government-friendly constituencies (i.e. middle-class *bazaari* bourgeoisie), public officials, and private corporations with firm ties to the state. Finally, close interaction with numerous subsidiaries in the private sector and social groups have strengthened the government's position in society by increasing its dependence on the state vis-à-vis wealth redistribution and oil rents. Still, the reinforcement of state power through oil rent expenditures has had an adverse effect on the state's proposed policy of reducing oil dependency.

---

[124] See: Brumberg, Daniel and Ariel Ahram. *The National Iranian Oil Company in Iranian Politics.* The James A. Baker III Institute for Public Policy, Rice University, 2007, p.18.

[125] Brumberg, Daniel and Ariel Ahram. *The National Iranian Oil Company in Iranian Politics.* The James A. Baker III Institute for Public Policy, Rice University, 2007, p. 19.

Ultimately, extensive nationalization projects in large sectors of the oil, banking and industrial sector greatly reduced the role of the private sector. Nationalization was justified by citing the need for social equality within an Islamic context with the state being the sole authority responsible for the enforcement and distribution of morality, justice, and the welfare of the general population. As a result, state-owned enterprises in the various sectors have typically incurred heavy debts, costs and bloated pay-rolls because of the numerous services and subsidies they offer citizens at practically no charge.[126] These costs have mostly been financed by external oil rents, which have actually increased the state's oil dependency.

However, it is important to note that state-society interdependency has increased due to the rentier mentality prevailing in government institutions, religious parastatal foundations, state structures, and publicly controlled corporations. This has fostered a greater sense of collectivity and strengthened state structures. The increased amount of vested interest in the preservation of state stability and the status quo has provided the theocratic government in Tehran with a firm support platform contributing to its resiliency.

4.2 Political and Economic Developments

The increasingly active role of the state, coupled with significant economic difficulties, witnessed a period of productive decline immediately after the revolution. The first year of the revolution (1979/1980) experienced a considerable reduction of industrial output and oil production (see table 2), whereas the agricultural and service sectors were the only areas that demonstrated growth. The sharp drop in the industrial sector resulted in a high unemployment rate and rising inflation. By 1980/81, oil exports reported a drop of 65.8% compared to the preceding year due to Western sanctions imposed because of the seizure of the American Embassy in Tehran within nine months of the revolution and by the Iraqi invasion and occupation of the *Shatt al Arab* territory in September 1980. Following the state's consolidation of power, the economy began a period of expansion in 1982/83. It posted an overall GDP growth rate of 14.4%, while the oil and agriculture sectors expanded by 120.7% and 7.1%, respectively. Amid high global oil prices, the positive growth trend continued in most sectors until the oil price shock in 1986, which reduced the overall

[126] See: Brumberg, Daniel and Ariel Ahram. *The National Iranian Oil Company in Iranian Politics.* The James A. Baker III Institute for Public Policy, Rice University, 2007, p.19.

GDP growth rate to -8.8% in 1986/87. However, overall GDP growth did not necessarily indicate positive internal developments. During the recovery period of 1981-1984, there was a widening gap between the rich and poor. Sohrab Behdad notes that "the ratio of expenditures of the wealthiest to that of the poorest 20 per cent of urban households, which had declined from 14.7 in 1977 to 9.1 in 1980, increased to 11.4 in 1984."[127] The scarcity of food and other products due to state rationing and international sanctions as a consequence of the war profited the black market while "benefits from government licensing of activities and outright corruption were increasing."[128]

Table 1: Macroeconomic Development and Sectoral Change

Year	1979/80	1980/81	1981/82	1982/83	1983/84	1984/85	1985/86	1986/87	1987/88	1988/89
Agriculture										
Growth rate	5.9	3.4	1.9	7.1	4.8	7.3	7.8	4.4	2.4	-2.5
Share in GDP	14.0	17.4	21.1	20.0	17.9	19.7	20.4	23.9	25.4	23.8
Oil										
Growth rate	-19.4	-65.8	1.9	120.7	3.0	-18.9	1.1	-14.7	13.9	9.7
Share in GDP	25.4	12.6	12.3	18.6	15.2	11.6	9.8	4.1	4.6	4.5
Industry										
Growth rate	-15.7	5.6	0.04	0.5	19.6	4.8	-5.5	-8.9	2.5	-5.0
Share in GDP	15.9	19.0	18.4	18.0	19.6	19.4	17.8	17.6	17.2	17.2
Services										
Growth rate	2.5	-2.2	-7.2	0.8	13.0	2.4	2.1	-13.3	-6.7	-7.1
Share in GDP	44.7	51.0	48.2	43.4	47.3	49.2	52.0	54.4	52.8	54.5
Gross domestic product (factor cost)										
Growth rate	-5.2	-14.9	-2.1	14.4	11.4	0.04	1.7	-8.8	0.4	-3.6

Note: The percentages of real growth over the year are at constant 1982/83 prices and the share in GDP and factor cost at 1993 prices.

Source: Bank Markazi: *Iran's National Accounts* 1353-1366 (1974/75-1987/88); *Iran's National Accounts* 1367-1669 (1988/89-1990/91); and *Annual Review*, 1991/92.
Amuzegar, Jahangir. *Iran's Economy Under the Islamic Republic*. New York and London: I. B. Tauris, 1993.

[127] Rahnema, Saeed and Sohrab Behdad (eds.) *Iran After The Revolution: Crisis Of An Islamic State.* London and New York: I.B. Taurius, 1995, p. 108.
[128] Ibid., p. 109.

The onset of the Iraq-Iran war in 1980 proved to be both a significant challenge and a hidden blessing for Khomeini's government. At that time, the Iranian army had approximately one hundred thousand troops at its disposal, a mere quarter of its pre-revolutionary size. With a depleted arms arsenal and low morale due to recent domestic turbulences, Khomeini nevertheless used the opportunity to retaliate against Saddam Hussein and his forces and reinforce his domestic power and authority. By rejecting Iraqi demands to cede the *Shatt al Arab* territory (of which the oil-rich Khuzestan province is a part of), Khomeini decided to seize this opportunity to rally Iranians of all classes to defend their country. In light of the external threat and the subsequent invasion of Iraqi troops into Iranian territory, a new upsurge of patriotic sentiments, and Khomeini's declaration that Saddam wanted to "war with Islam", he succeeded in uniting the general masses against Iraq. By 1982, the newly bolstered Iranian military managed to retake their occupied territories from the Iraqis and drove the foreign troops back to the previous international border. Meanwhile, Iran refused various efforts by the United Nations to negotiate a truce with Iraq because its demands of removing Saddam Hussein from power and a $150 billion war compensation package would not be met. Khomeini used the rejection of its demands by the UN as a front to continue the war, knowing that as long as an exogenous threat to Iran existed, he would be able to further strengthen the state's position internally.

In spite of reduced external oil profits, the Iranian state managed to consolidate its power and maintain domestic stability by a number of other means. It boosted morale among the populace by "presenting the conflict as one between believers and the infidel Baathist regime, which, by its own admission, was secular."[129] In addition, the decline in the productive sectors due to the war necessitated the heavy subsidization and rationing of food supplies. "Since rationing imposed equality in consumption, it helped the government to portray itself as egalitarian."[130] Meanwhile, Iran's industries also managed to reap benefits from the war. Because of heavy import restrictions regarding arms and military equipment, the Iranian government imported used spare-parts for U.S.-made weapons from Vietnam, where large leftover caches from the American-Vietnam War were still to be

---

[129] Hiro, Dilip. *Iran Today*. London: Politico's Publishing, 2006, p.221.
[130] Ibid., p.222.

found. Also, the state expanded its tax extraction capacity over the next few years in order to diversify its source of revenue, provide funding for the war and compensate for lost oil profits due to declining oil prices and international sanctions. Due to the disorder and turmoil caused by the revolution, the state only accrued 4.4 billion rial in indirect taxes as of 1980. After the start of the war, the state's revenues in net indirect taxes jumped to 146.2 billion rial, with the numbers rapidly rising over the next few years. During the oil price shock of 1986, where the global oil price fell to about $10 a barrel, the government posted 555.5 billion rial in indirect tax profits for 1986/87, and a war-time high of 602.7 billion rial in the following year. The extension of the state's tax extraction capabilities during times of scarce oil profits and war proved to be beneficial for Iran's authoritarian government. Benjamin Smith asserts that "the extraction of taxes entails making decisions about from whom and how to acquire (the) money and politicizes those decisions by mandating bargaining with social groups over the representation-taxation equation, which generates revenues as it builds patterns of interaction between state and society. Thus, not only the information engendered by a robust tax bureaucracy but also the consequent capacity to keep an eye on social groups powerfully affects an authoritarian state's ability to exercise social control."[131]

Table 2: Iranian Net Indirect Taxes 1979-1989

Year	**Net Indirect Taxes** (In billions of rial) At current prices
1979/80	4,4
1980/81	146,2
1981/82	113,3
1982/83	185,2
1983/84	404,4
1984/85	508,7
1985/86	550,6
1986/87	555,5
1987/88	602,7
1988/89	498,9

Source: Bank Markazi Jomhuri-ye Eslami-ye Iran. *Economic Report and Balance Sheet*, various issues.

[131] Smith, Benjamin. *Hard Times in the Lands of Plenty: Oil Politics in Iran and Indonesia.* Ithaca, NY: Cornell University Press, 2007, p.52.

The Iraqi incursions and attacks caused considerable damage to the Abadan oil refinery, nearly totally destroyed the largest Iranian port city of Khorramshahr, and reduced both agricultural and industrial production in the occupied territories in the south and west.[132] Still, the loss of Iran's oil supplies to the international market caused by the revolution and sanctions pushed the price of one barrel of oil from $13 to $20 dollars. Even with the reduction of oil output from 3.3 mb/d in 1979 to 1.4 mb/d, Iran earned more because of the price hikes (see table 4). So, with the resumption of exports at 1.3 mb/d in 1981, Iran continued to earn more than before while producing less. For instance, Iran had an almost equal oil output of about 2.5 mb/d in 1984 and 1986, but earned $16.7 and $ 6.2 billion, respectively. Thus, the steady oil output average made the state extremely susceptible to external price boom and bust cycles. However, the profits reaped by the Iranian state despite lowered or equal oil output suggests that oil and hydrocarbon resources could be employed as strategic tools to influence global markets and place economic pressure on other states.

Table 3: Iranian Oil Production 1979-1989

Year	**Oil Production** (Thousand barrels daily)
1979	3218
1980	1479
1981	1321
1982	2397
1983	2454
1984	2043
1985	2205
1986	2054
1987	2342
1988	2349
1989	2894

Source: BP Statistical Review of World Energy Full Report 2007

The destabilization of the international oil market caused by the war, internal political instability due to conflicting factions, and the disruptions in Iranian oil output pushed the dollar price of a barrel of oil to nearly $40 (see figure 3). By 1982, oil exports

[132] Vast oil fields were discovered in the city of Abadan in the Khuzestan province during the early 1900's. To this day, it remains an important city with large facilities for the refinement of petroleum in the IRI.

constituted 98% of Iran's foreign revenues, indicating the state's heavy dependence on petroleum exports.

Figure 3: World Nominal Oil Price Chronology 1970-2006

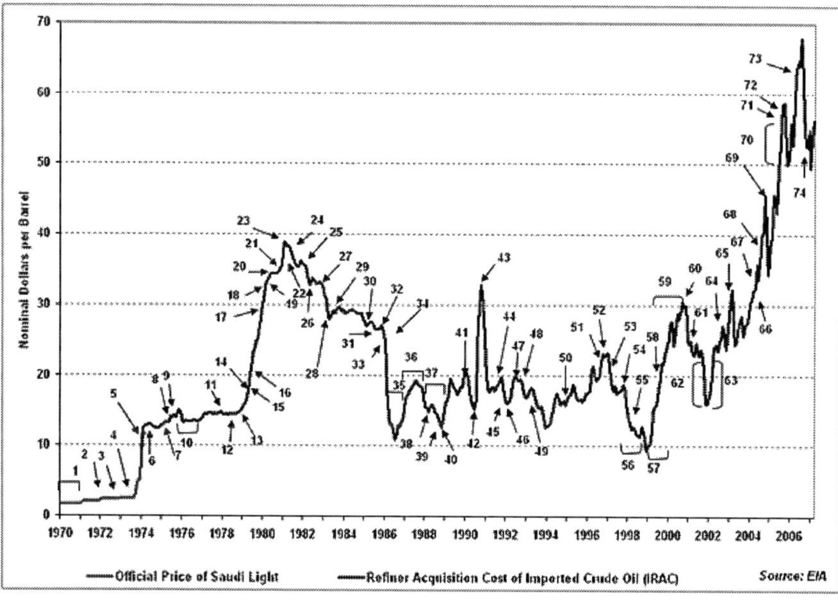

Source: Energy Information Administration (EIA) 2007

The years 1982/83 marked a period of growth in real output and public confidence and the restoration of partial political stability in the IRI. Khomeini's initial endorsement of president Bani-Sadr proved to be detrimental to the interests of religious hardliners. Instead of fulfilling a moderating role to maintain political balance between clerics and religious non-clerics, Bani-Sadr "made no effort to reach a modus vivendi with the senior clerics who set up the IRP with the blessing of Khomeini."[133] Amidst serious economic woes in 1981, Bani-Sadr blamed Khomeini's government and the IRP dominated parliament (or *Majlis*) for the last three years of economic recession, their inability to provide security, bureaucratic inconsistencies and disorder, and ineffective national policies. The presentation of information to Khomeini in April of 1981 linking Bani-Sadr with the Central Intelligence Agency (CIA)

[133] Hiro, Dilip. *Iran Today*. London: Politico's Publishing, 2006, p.133.

of the U.S. in Paris and later in Tehran, prompted hardliners to take action against the president. The *Majlis* subsequently impeached Bani-Sadr by 177 votes to one on June 20, 1981. By marginalizing political rivals from both the secular-moderate and radical-left factions, Khomeini's Islamic party was able to consolidate its power further over the state apparatus and extensive religious networks. The following four years sparked a recovery period in which oil production was resumed amidst relatively stable global crude prices. In 1983, the oil sector experienced an increase of a whopping 120% to the previous year, with overall annual oil revenues amounting to $23 billion. The average annual real growth rate posted a 6.9% increase, albeit from a low base.[134] This positive growth trend was brought to a halt during the stalemate in the war from 1984-86, during which Iraq escalated its assault on Iranian oil tankers and oil terminals. The attacks on oil production facilities, the loss of oil profits, massive war expenditures and depleted foreign exchange resources led to a 9.3% annual drop in GDP in 1986 (see table 4).

Table 4: Selected Data on the Economy of the IRI (1980-1989)

Subject Description	Units	Scale	1980	1981	1982	1983	1984	1985	1986	1987	1988	19
Current Account Balance	Billions	US Dollars	-3.5	-4.3	4.9	-0.4	-0.9	-0.3	-5.6	-2.6	-2.1	-2.
Current Account Balance in % of GDP		Ratio	-3.8	-4.1	3.7	-0.3	-0.6	-1.2	-6.8	-2.8	-2.5	-3.
GDP per capita, current prices		US Dollars	2445	2609	3140	3676	3664	1670	1685	1894	1621	15
GDP, constant prices, annual % change		Percent	-14.9	7.9	14.4	10.3	3.3	4.2	-9.3	-2.2	-14.1	6.2
GDP, current prices	Billions	US Dollars	93.7	106.5	133.3	162.4	168.4	79.8	83.3	95.9	84.1	81
Inflation		Index 2000=100	2.1	2.6	3.1	3.8	4.2	4.4	5.5	7.0	9.1	10
Inflation,		Percent	20.6	24.2	18.7	19.7	12.6	4.4	23.7	27.7	28.9	17

[134] See: Amuzegar, Jahangir. *Iran's Economy Under the Islamic Republic*. New York and London: I. B. Tauris, 1993, p. 51.
Amuzegar also notes that real GDP in 1985/86 was still below that of 1977/78.

annual percentage change												

Source: International Monetary Fund (IMF) *World Economic Outlook Database*, 2007.

Furthermore, the price of oil fell from $28 to less than $10 a barrel due to the flooding of the market by Saudi Arabia and Kuwait. With petroleum exports averaging 1.6 mb/d, Iran's oil revenues plunged from $13.7 billion in 1985 to $6.2 billion in 1986.

Table 5: Balance of Payments 1977-1988 (US$ million)

	1977	**1980**	**1984**	**1985**	**1986**	**1987**	**1988**
Exports, merchandise	21,521	12,338	17,087	14,175	7171	11,916	10,709
Oil and gas	20,926	11,693	16,726	13,710	6266	10,755	9673
Non-oil products	595	645	361	465	916	1161	1036
Imports, merchandise	-17,968	-10,888	-14,494	-12,006	-10,585	-12,005	-10,608
Intermediate and capital goods (%)	(82)	(73)	(84)	(86)	(82)	(82)	(82)
Trade balance	3553	1450	2593	2169	-3414	-89	101
Current-account balance	1293	-2434	1924	-476	-5156	-2090	-1869

Source: Bank Markazi Jomhuri-ye Eslami-ye Iran. *Economic Report and Balance Sheet*, various issues.

The drop in oil prices affected the incomes of most oil-exporting states, including Iraq. But, whereas external oil rents were the principal form of income for the IRI the previous year, they only constituted 4% in the GDP share in 1986/87. Iraq, in contrast, enjoyed an additional $12 billion in foreign aid from its allies in the West, the Gulf States and the Soviet Union. This was to have far-reaching implications for the course of the war. The annual inflation percentage change increased from 4.4% in 1985 to 23.7% in 1986. International isolation and reduced government funds for subsidies drove up domestic food prices, limited foreign imports, and consequently caused increased domestic unrest. Instead of formulating policies to ease the economic strain, the Iranian government encouraged more participation for the war. The *Bonyad-e Shahid* played a key role in maintaining morale among the populace by providing social and financial services for the family members of military personnel. Families of dead soldiers received generous financial compensations and benefits, thus creating incentives for the new generation of Iranian youths to join the military. The limitation of the state's expenditure capacity forced it to employ alternative means of mobilizing the masses while simultaneously building crucial social networks to channel social discontent away from the government. By blending Islam with war, Khomeini was able to rally enough volunteers to his cause without having to drastically increase military expenditures. This coalition-building and socio-political reinforcement process proved to be an important factor in keeping the government's power and administrative structure intact while facing exogenous threats and fiscal scarcity. Although the strengthening of state-society relations as a consequence of external threats and difficult economic times enabled the Iranian state to sustain itself and establish relative stability domestically, increasing U.S. military involvement and international aid provided to Iraq prevented it from making any conclusive or decisive gains concerning the war. The overwhelming material and financial resources Iraq had at its disposal coupled with a series of military setbacks ultimately forced the IRI to unconditionally accept UN Security Council Resolution 598 on July 18, 1988, which called for a ceasefire and an end to all military actions.[135] As Dilip Hiro aptly puts it, "the war enabled Khomeini to mobilize Iranians, religious and secular, on a patriotic platform, and have his own often fractious followers sink their differences on how to run the country, especially the economy. Conscious of the cementing effect of the war, he repeatedly rejected offers of mediation and a ceasefire. Had Saddam not invaded Iran, it was likely that the fledgling Islamic republic would have slipped into civil war. The Iraqi President could therefore be perceived as an inadvertent contributor to the consolidation of the Islamic revolution in Iran."[136]

---

[135] According to the Stockholm International Peace Research Institute (SIPRI), Iraq acquired over $40 billion in military imports compared to Iran's $11.2 billion. Moreover, The Economist in 1987 estimated huge imbalances in military capabilities, with the Iraqis possessing 4,500 tanks, 500+ aircraft, 150 helicopters, and 4000+ artillery versus Iran's respective totals of 1000, 65, 60, and 1000+.

[136] Hiro, Dilip. *Iran Today*. London: Politico's Publishing, 2006, p.234.

5. PHASE II: 1989-1997, ISLAMIC ECONOMIC LIBERALIZATION

The end of the Iran-Iraq war in 1988 followed by Khomeini's death in June 1989 signalled the beginning of a new phase of developments in the IRI. Contrary to many pessimistic predictions, the passing of the charismatic leader of the Islamic Revolution did not result in an ensuing internal power struggle. In 1989, Iranians voted for a constitutional amendment that introduced a new system of executive presidency and dispensed with the post of prime minister because it hindered efficient administration. Ali Akbar Hashemi Rafsanjani, a pragmatic "modern-rightist" politician, was voted in as the new president of Iran by a plurality of 95% with a voter turnout of approximately 14.2 million.[137] In the same year, the former president and close confidante of Ayatollah Khomeini, Ali Khamenei, a strict traditionalist conservative, was elected by the *Majlis-e Khebregan* (Assembly of Experts) to become Supreme Leader of the IRI. The smooth transition of power and general unity among the populace (which can partly be attributed to the unifying effect of exogenous threats/factors such as the war with Iraq, international sanctions, and the containment strategy of Western powers) marked a period of relative political stability that presented President Rafsanjani's administration with the opportunity to introduce new policies designed to revive the ailing economy.

Rafsanjani's initial domestic liberalization efforts were backed by both the *bazaaris* and the social conservatives in the *Majlis*, who stood to directly profit from the newly proposed policies. Full support gradually waned as Rafsanjani's implemented liberalization reforms also included the restructuring of Iran's foreign exchange guidelines as well as promoting greater foreign direct investment and trade by making the Iranian domestic market more accessible internationally. The prospects of foreign involvement and giving up a share of Iran's economy did not sit well with conservatives and hardliners in the *Majlis*. It also met with disapproval in the Assembly of Experts and Supreme Leader Ali Khamenei, who wanted to maintain their firm control over the domestic market. Pragmatic businessmen and entrepreneurs, in contrast, welcomed the state's liberalization and reform efforts, and were clearly satisfied with the prospects of increasing profits and gaining greater access to foreign markets and goods. The rise of the leftist faction and the moderate

[137] See: Hiro, Dilip. *Iran Today*. London: Politico's Publishing, 2006, p. 45.

supporters of their agenda in the third session of the *Majlis* (1988-1992) presented President Rafsanjani with the opportunity to gain the backing of religious hardliners. As both leftists and their moderate allies in the *Majlis* actively resisted Rafsanjani's reform proposals, the president opted to collaborate with the Supreme Leader Khamenei and his conservative allies to curtail their power and ensure their defeat in the next elections. As it was in the mutual interest of both parties to marginalize the leftist camp, Khamenei agreed to back Rafsanjani and his reform policies in the next parliamentary elections of 1992 and the presidential elections of 1993. The opportunistic and temporary alliance of traditional and "modern-right" conservatives succeeded in revising the constitution in favor of a stronger presidency and a more powerful Supreme Leader. This ultimately led to the defeat of the leftist faction in the 1992 *Majlis*, where a number of their candidates were barred by the Guardian Council from running in the elections, and paved the way for the alliance of conservatives to pursue their political interests.

The introduction of the first Five Year Plan (1989-1994) reflected President Rafsanjani's more pragmatic and less ideological approach aimed at reconstructing the economy. A series of liberalization and reform policies were put into effect in order to promote private investment and privatization, introduce alternative foreign exchange and trade policies, curb increasing inflation rates, reduce the budget deficit, improve the oil and industrial sectors, and aid in the reconstruction of regions damaged by the war. These policies demonstrated positive initial developments due to favorable economic conditions, but exhibited significant flaws over the five-year course of the plan that had negative consequences for the Iranian domestic market.

5.1 Political and Economic Developments

The early concerted efforts of the state in 1989 to develop various sectors of the economy after the debilitating eight-year war with Iraq were met with initial success. As illustrated in tables 6 and 7, the expansion of various productive sectors led to a 4.2% increase in GDP in 1989/90 and a nominal GDP jump from $81.2 billion (in current prices) in 1989 to $97.3 billion in 1991. By 1990/91, improvements undertaken in the oil and industrial sectors, the liberalization of trade and foreign exchange policies and increased foreign imports accompanied by a surge in private consumption expenditures all boosted the GDP by 11.5%, with oil exports constituting 19.9% of overall GDP.[138] An increase in raw material and machinery imports improved industrial growth from 6.6% in 1989/90 to a high of 17.2% in 1991/92. The GDP per capita during the outset of the first Five Year Plan also saw a steady rise from $1526 in 1989 to a peak of $1864 in 1992, sparking a rise in consumer confidence. Consequently, enhanced consumer confidence contributed to increased domestic spending, which further added to the average annual GDP growth rate of 7.3% over the five year period (1989-1994). In 1990/91, private consumption expenditures grew by a rate of 19.5% compared to the previous years' rate of a mere 2.5%. The distribution of foreign imports skyrocketed from $8.1 billion in 1988/89 to $18.7 billion in 1991/92. Also, improvements were achieved in the areas of education, where spending in 1992 reached a record high of nearly 30% of total government expenditures. Yet, this still only amounted to approximately 5% of overall GDP.[139]

Figure 4: IRI Education Expenditures (1980-2006)

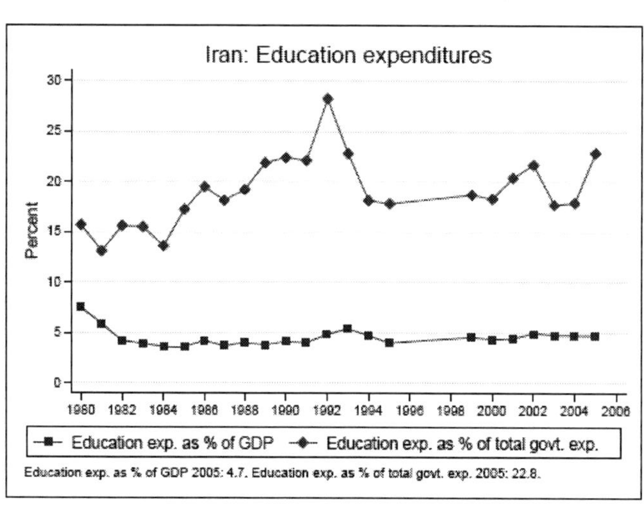

Source: UNICEF. *Division of Policy and Planning, Strategic Information Section*. 2007. www.childinfo.org

[138] For a detailed account, see: Pesaran, Hashem. "Economic Trends and Macroeconomic Policies," in Alizadeh, Parvin (ed.) *"The Economy of Iran: Dilemmas of an Islamic State."* London and New York: I.B. Tauris, 2000, p. 68.

[139] The government expenditures for education in relation to the overall GDP can be attributed to the high price of oil in 1991.

Table 6: Selected Data on the Economy of the IRI (1989-1997)

Subject Description	Units	Scale	1989	1990	1991	1992	1993	1994	1995	1996	1997
Current Account Balance	Billion	US Dollars	-2.9	-2.6	-11.2	-7.3	-4.2	5.0	3.3	5.2	2.2
Current Account Balance in % of GDP		Ratio	-3.7	-3.2	-11.5	-6.4	-4.9	7.5	3.7	4.7	2.1
GDP per capita, current prices		US Dollars	1526	1523	1743	1864	1407	1084	1446	1769	1745
GDP, constant prices, annual % change		Percent	6.2	16.9	15.2	4.3	-1.6	-0.4	2.7	7.1	3.4
GDP, current prices	Billion	US Dollars	81.2	83.0	97.3	114.7	85.8	67.0	90.8	110.6	106.3
Inflation		Index 2000=100	10.6	11.6	14.0	17.4	21.4	29.0	43.3	53.3	62.6
Inflation, annual percentage change		Percent	17.4	9.0	20.6	24.4	22.9	35.2	49.4	23.2	17.3

Source: International Monetary Fund (IMF) *World Economic Outlook Database*, 2007.

Table 7: Actual Sectoral Output Growths During the First Five-Year Plan 1989-1994 (percentage)

Sectors	1989/90	1990/91	1991/92	1992/93	1993/94	1989-1994 Average Growth
Agriculture	3.7	8.1	5.1	7.4	5.5	5.9
Industries and Mines	6.6	13.4	17.2	4.7	1.3	8.7
Water, gas, and Electricity	11.0	19.4	15.5	8.5	9.4	12.7
Construction	-1.7	2.9	16.0	7.9	2.4	5.5
Services	1.8	9.7	9.9	8.0	7.5	7.4
Oil	7.7	19.9	11.1	2.1	3.6	8.9
GDP	4.2	11.5	10.1	6.0	4.8	7.3

Source: *Bank Markazi Jomhuri Islami Iran*. Actual figures are based on gross domestic product at factor cost in constant 1982/1983 prices.

See: Pesaran, Hashem. "Economic Trends and Macroeconomic Policies," in Alizadeh, Parvin (ed.) *"The Economy of Iran: Dilemmas of an Islamic State."* London and New York: I.B. Tauris, 2000, p.67.

However, the perceived initial economic success of the first Five Year Plan demonstrated serious deficits and discrepancies in Iran's patterns of development. Sectoral output growths (as illustrated in table 7) heavily relied on the performance of the oil sector. The invasion of Kuwait by Iraqi forces in August 1990 pushed crude prices up from around $17 a barrel to over $30, with oil production increasing from around 2.8 mb/d in 1989 to 3.5 mb/d in 1991. By 1990/91, the oil sector had a 19.9% growth output compared to 7.7% in the previous year. Consequently, all other sectors registered an increase in output, with industry/mines, water/gas/electricity and services posting the most obvious gains. As oil growth output declined to 2.1% in 1992/93, so too did output decrease in every other sector except agriculture.

Table 8: Iranian Oil Production 1990-1997

Year	**Oil Production** (Thousand barrels daily)
1990	3270
1991	3500
1992	3523
1993	3712
1994	3730
1995	3744
1996	3759
1997	3776

Source: BP Statistical Review of World Energy Full Report 2007

Also, "the high growth achieved during the first half of the plan largely reflected the initial effects of the trade and foreign exchange liberalization and utilization of unused capacity in the economy, and was accompanied by an unprecedented surge in private consumption expenditures."[140] Once these capacities were used up, output growths started to dwindle.[141] Rafsanjani's pursuit of a more liberal economic policy increased competition, privatized national enterprises, decreased state subsidies, and unified Iran's exchange rate policy in 1993 with the aim to increase production and profitability, reduce the dependence on imports, increase exports and contain

[140] Alizadeh, Parvin. *"The Economy of Iran: Dilemmas of an Islamic State."* London and New York, I.B. Tauris, 2000, p.68.
[141] These capacities quickly met their full potential because of the lack of productive emphasis and poor industrial and manufacturing infrastructures in Iran's economic sectors (i.e. industry, construction, etc.).

consumption growth.[142] The foreign exchange realignment policy was a key aspect of his liberalization efforts, designed to boost domestic industrial output and lessen Iran's reliance on foreign imports. Because the rial's high value had been artificially maintained in the preceding years, its overvaluation had negative effects on the economy. Sorhab Behdad asserts that the overvalued exchange rate policy made it possible for Iran "to run a highly import-dependent industrial structure and to minimize, at least in the short-run, the deterioration of the standards of living of the Iranian population."[143] In the long-run, however, its strong value had cheapened the inflow of imports and caused a decline in the market share of domestic Iranian industries, in effect reducing the output capacities of various crucial sectors. At the same time, the heavy dependence on foreign imports increased the IRI's foreign exchange deficit. The devaluation of the rial in 1993 and the adoption of a floating currency were meant to have a positive effect on the foreign-exchange deficit by decreasing foreign imports while increasing export earnings. But, because most of Iran's exports have large import content and their net foreign exchange profit is less than their export value indicates, the devaluation of the rial did not succeed in reducing foreign imports. Moreover, the main export product of the IRI, namely oil, is unaffected by exchange-rate changes, thus the devaluation policy of Rafsanjani's administration was only minimally effective and hardly succeeded in reducing the foreign exchange gap.[144] Meanwhile, increased foreign loans (used to finance the skyrocketing costs of imports caused by the devaluation of currency) and subsequent debts incurred over the five-year period caused the annual inflation rate to rise from 9.0% in 1990 to 35.2% in 1994. High inflation rates and the reduction of state subsidies particularly affected salaried civil servants and soldiers in the military, both key groups which significantly contribute to state stability in the IRI. The national account balance continued to register deficits during the first Five Year Plan, reaching a peak of -$11.2 billion in 1991, despite considerable oil profits in the same year. This was due to the excessive and unchecked consumer consumption of

[142] The state unified the exchange rates by floating the rial from $1= IR 70 and $1=IR 600 to a "float" of $1=IR 1542.
[143] Rahnema, Saeed and Sohrab Behdad (eds.) *Iran After The Revolution: Crisis Of An Islamic State*. London and New York: I.B. Taurius, 1995, p.116.
[144] Sorhab Behdad notes that oil is unaffected by exchange rate changes because its prices are determined in dollars in the international market and because the volume of Iran's exports of oil depend on international market considerations, not by the rial cost of production of oil.
See: Rahnema, Saeed and Sohrab Behdad (eds.) *Iran After The Revolution: Crisis Of An Islamic State*. London and New York: I.B. Taurius, 1995, p.127.

imports and Iran's own limited capacity to export. High foreign indebtedness and the World Bank's inability to provide financial aid due to the threat of U.S. vetoes caused a currency crisis in 1993, resulting in the sharp depreciation of the rial by 95%. By 1994, the rial had dropped to $1=IR 2850, consequently forcing the state and the Bank Markazi to retake control of the foreign-exchange market, re-establish policies of foreign trade restrictions, reduce imports, and fix exchange rates.

The first Five Year Plan's overly optimistic growth objectives had failed to materialize. The source of the state's optimism was largely rooted in its confidence of steadily rising prospective oil revenues. But, as profits declined due to an unexpected decrease in global oil prices, the state could not maintain its planned public domestic expenditures and simultaneously pay off its foreign debts and trade deficits. Thus, oil price volatility was also a major cause of disruptions in public spending and hindered efficient, long-term economic investment projects. Rafsanjani's liberalization reforms resulted in substantial balance of payment deficits, increased urban unemployment due to a reduction in the size of government bureaucracy, a slowdown of economic growth, depressed living standards (the GDP per capita plummeted from $1526 in 1989 to $1084 in 1994), high inflation rates, and an untimely and badly organized unification of the foreign exchange. In addition, Amuzegar notes that there was "a notable shift of resources (including labor) from more productive endeavors to low-value-added activities in the overcrowded and highly inefficient services."[145] The shift of resources to the service sector indicated some key characteristics of a rentier state. Because bureaucracies in the service sector often have an allocative function, they did not experience extreme fluctuations in developmental patterns. External rents accrued mostly from oil revenues by the Iranian state had to be redistributed to the domestic population, which largely occurred through the service sector. But, the decline in oil revenues could not accommodate the booming population growth of the IRI. Since 1979, the population had increased from 37.7 million to 63.5 million in 1994; real GDP, conversely, remained about the same as the pre-revolution level. A decline in per capita income and private consumption further exacerbated Iran socio-economically, increasing general disenchantment among the populace concerning the state's economic liberalization reforms. The negative impact of the liberalization policy also increased both factional conflicts and political opposition to the state. The

[145] Amuzegar, Jahangir. *Iran's Economy Under the Islamic Republic*. New York and London: I. B. Tauris, 1993, p.60.

initial aura of optimism created by economic growth was replaced by discontent targeting the disproportionate distribution of wealth, growing corruption, and opulence among Islamic clerics and leaders, a reality which was far removed from the idealistic slogans of equal wealth distribution and equality for all preceding the revolution in 1979.

The lack of significant exogenous threats and the death of a charismatic and authoritative figure like Ayatollah Khomeini provided few tools for the theocratic government to consolidate its power internally. Throughout the 1990's, President Clinton's "dual-containment" policy attempted to isolate Iran and Iraq from the international community in an attempt to weaken their positions politically and economically. In particular, it sought to prohibit the expansion of Iranian influence in the Middle East through regional alliances, economic sanctions, and a heavy U.S. military presence in the Gulf. A series of U.S.-sponsored international sanctions were imposed on the IRI, including:

- the freezing of loans from the World Bank in 1994,
- President Clinton's "Executive Order 12957 (March 15, 1995), which banned U.S. investment in Iran's energy sector, and Executive Order 12959 (May 6, 1995), which banned U.S. trade with and investment in that country,"[146] and
- the Iran-Libya Sanctions Act (ILSA) of 1996, which imposed sanctions on foreign companies that would make new investments of at least $40 million in Iran.

"The Clinton Administration and many in Congress maintained that the new U.S. sanctions might begin to deprive Iran of the ability to acquire weapons of mass destruction (WMD) and fund terrorist groups by hindering its ability to modernize its key source of revenue -- the petroleum sector."[147] The pursuit of the "dual-containment" policy was justified by accusing the IRI of sponsoring international terrorism, hindering peace and security in the Middle East, and developing weapons of mass destruction (it had recently signed a contract with Russia in 1995 for the construction of a nuclear power reactor at Bushehr). However, the policy of international sanctions and isolation against the IRI proved to be largely ineffective. Many countries like Japan and Russia were not willing to abide by the restrictions,

---

[146] Katzman, Kenneth. "The Iran-Libya Sanctions Act (ILSA)," in *Library of Congress, Washington D.C. Congressional Research Service,* July 20, 2001.
http://stinet.dtic.mil/oai/oai?&verb=getRecord&metadataPrefix=html&identifier=ADA475995
[147] Ibid.

due to the opportunity for lucrative trade relations provided by President Rafsanjani's recent economic liberalization reforms. The U.S.'s strict containment and sanctions policies during the 1980's, conversely, proved to be much more effective. At the time, Iran's domestic market, still reeling from the revolutionary turmoil of 1979 and heavily burdened by the war, could not provide an attractive economic venue for foreign investment and trade. Thus, the international sanctions imposed in the 1980's were enforced and widely supported by the majority of the international community, which put significant economic and political pressure on the IRI. This is why Ayatollah Khomeini was able to exploit the U.S.'s uncompromising stance towards the Islamic Republic by making Washington responsible for Iran's difficult plight. In comparison, the U.S. strategy towards the IRI during the 1990's was relatively mild and provided little fodder for Tehran's clerics to use as propaganda to shift the focus of social dissent away from the state during times of economic and social hardship. Also, the liberalization of Iran's economy exposed its society to the effects of globalization. The increased exchange of goods and services, information, and ideas provided the populace with the opportunity to attain greater insight into the state of affairs in other countries. In comparison to its prosperous, oil-rich neighbors, the IRI's economic plight appeared relatively dismal. This exacerbated domestic dissatisfaction and resulted in social unrest and political cleavages in the aftermath of economic setbacks and the foreign exchange crisis.

In 1993, President Rafsanjani's run for re-election was successful (mainly due to the support of Khamenei and his conservative allies), albeit at a reduced margin of victory and a much lower turnout than was the case in 1989.[148] In order to quell internal unrest among crucial social groups, his administration decided to rely more heavily on the state's coercive appeasement capacity (i.e. "buying" loyalty through patronage networks, higher allowances for public servants, decreased extraction of indirect taxes, state subsidies for foodstuffs and fuel, etc.); state apparatuses such as the Guardian Council were utilized to disperse and eliminate opposition from the political stage. However, violent social protests in 1995, initiated by the poorer classes and the *mostazafan*, targeted the negative economic developments of the

---

[148] Rafsanjani received 65% of the vote on a voter turnout of 56%. Of 270 deputies, only 79 were re-elected, whereas those who were considered "unreformed" were either disqualified or not elected.
See: Rahnema, Saeed and Sohrab Behdad (eds.) *Iran After The Revolution: Crisis Of An Islamic State.* London and New York: I.B. Taurius, 1995, p.122.

past five years and resulted in increased public pressure.[149] Realizing that the drastic economic situation had the potential to generate violent mass protests, the government took immediate action to improve economic conditions. Once again, the country's economic predicament topped the agenda of Rafsanjani's second presidential term. Through the proposition of his second Five Year Plan (1994-1999), Rafsanjani's administration decided to adopt an interventionist role for the state concerning economic affairs. By re-establishing a more assertive role, the state hoped to alleviate the economic impacts of the liberalization policy of the first Five Year Plan. In light of soaring inflation rates, trade deficits and a rapidly progressing foreign exchange crisis, the government partially abandoned its liberalization policies and imposed foreign exchange controls, trade restrictions, and strict credit controls. Over the next few years, this resulted in a reduction of foreign imports and a steady average output of non-oil exports.

Table 9: Balance of Payments (million US dollars)

	1989/90	**1990/91**	**1991/92**	**1992/93**	**1993/94**	**1994/95**	**1995/96**	**1996/97**
Trade Balance	-367	975	-6,529	-3,406	-1,207	6,817	5,586	7,402
Exports	13,081	19,305	18,661	19,868	18,080	19,434	18,360	22,391
Oil and Gas	(12,037)	(17,993)	(16,012)	(16,880)	(14,333)	(14,603)	(15,103)	(19,271)
Others	(1,044)	(1,312)	(2,649)	(2,988)	(3,747)	(4,831)	(3,257)	(3,120)
Imports	-13,448	-18,330	-25,190	-23,274	-19,287	-12,617	-12,774	-14,989

Source: *Annual Reviews*, 1991/92 (1370) and 1992/93 (1371), and *Economic Trends*, Economic Research Department, Bank Markazi Jomhuri Islami Iran, 1997.

The rise of oil prices from $15 a barrel in 1994 to over $20 a barrel in 1996 increased Iran's foreign exchange profits, bringing the total to $19.2 billion in that year and helped to reduce its national budget deficit. Furthermore, controls over public and private sector credits and the stabilization of the rial managed to reduce the annual

[149] The *mostazafan*, or "the oppressed", actually constituted the traditional public base of the religious Islamic faction and played a key role during the Islamic revolution of 1979. The Islamic state in Iran placed itself in the role of protector of the *mostazafan* and realized it had to take action when they participated in the protests of 1995.

inflation percentage change rate of 49.4% in 1995 to 23.3% in 1996. Also, the GDP per capita rose from a low of $1084 in 1994 to $1745 in 1997, which diverted at least some of the financial burden away from the working class over the short-term. However, Iran's import deficit could not be reduced and actually posted an increase from -$12.7 billion in 1995/96 to -$14.9 billion in 1996/97.

Rafsanjani's newly implemented strategy after 1994 did manage to achieve short-term output growth, reduce the national foreign debt deficit and slow down the annual inflation rate. However, he was able to attain these objectives due largely in part because of the stabilizing effect of consistent oil profits. These external rents provided the state with the additional revenues necessary to counteract the adverse effects of its currency devaluation policies, pay-off external debts, lessen the impact of social protests, and increase worker remittances amid soaring prices, high inflation and sinking per capita incomes. Higher wages offered added incentives to public servants and managed to create a certain degree of loyalty to the state. The rentier mentality in the IRI generated a complex form of patron-client exchanges that established multiple layers of rent recipients and increased interdependency between state and society, as well as strengthened the internal structures of government institutions. Furthermore, the multilayered structure of power in the IRI enabled the state to deflect the full brunt of mass protests by not providing a single and clear target. This is one aspect of the current state's capacity to cope with public dissent that differentiates it with the government in pre-revolutionary Iran. The widespread demonstrations and uprisings that led to the Islamic revolution of 1979 clearly were aimed at one principal figure, namely the Shah, who was deemed as the person responsible for all of Iran's economic, social and political woes.

6. PHASE III: 1997-2004, SOCIAL AND POLITICAL LIBERALIZATION PROCESS

The economic and social setbacks of Rafsanjani's liberalization reform policies prompted the Iranian electorate to vote for change in the 1997 presidential elections. Muhammad Khatami's landslide victory signified the populace's opposition to the imposition of traditionalist Islamic norms and the preservation of the status quo over the past 17 years. The results reflected their desire not only for economic, but also cultural and social change.[150] Being a political moderate and a cleric of high standing, Khatami appealed to a variety of factions including the "modern right," a liberal coalition promoting economic liberalism, the "modern left," the hard-core remainder of the populist-statist tendency, who dominated the IRI in the first decade after the 1979 revolution, as well as to women and the youth. He was favored by religious supporters because of his status as a *sayyid*, which conferred Khatami a higher rank than his political opponent Nateq-Nouri.[151] Khatami supported the Islamic revolution, firmly backed the constitution and emphasized the rule of law. He also advocated an Islamic system that supported a more open civil society, freedom of expression, improved international relations with other nations, the creation of more jobs (especially for the youth), and better opportunities for women and minorities.[152] But, this broad-based appeal also posed a major challenge to Khatami's presidency. His campaign for the presidency in 1997 was supported by two opposing political factions within the government, namely "a liberal coalition promoting economic liberalism and the hard-core remainders of the populist-statist tendency."[153] This meant that he had to play a balancing-act when it came to issues that did not appeal to both sides. In addition, because of the multiple centers of power in the Iranian

[150] The presidential elections took place on May 23, 1997 with a voter turnout of approximately 33 million. Khatami received nearly 69% of the vote, with Nateq-Nouri's receiving only 25%.

[151] *Sayyid* is a religious title bestowed upon males accepted as descendants of the Islamic prophet Muhammad. They are entitled to wear black turbans, signifying a higher rank than religious counterparts who don a white turban (as was the case with Nateq-Nouri).

[152] Population growth was encouraged after the 1979 revolution by political and religious leaders, particularly in the 1980s. Although this policy was abandoned during the 1990's, the population has continued to grow due to its momentum and dynamic nature. The population structure in Iran is such that a large proportion of the population will seek employment in the future, which explains Khatami's focus to specifically target job creation for the youth.
See: Valadkhani, A. "An Analysis of Iran's Third Five-Year Development Plan in the Post-Revolution Era (2000-2005)," in *Journal of Iranian Research and Analysis*, 17(2), 2001, and p.10.
http://ro.uow.edu.au/commpapers/399

[153] Alizadeh, Parvin. *"The Economy of Iran: Dilemmas of an Islamic State."* London and New York, I.B. Tauris, 2000, p.134.

state structure, Khatami would always have to consider the effect his policies would have on each institution.[154] Aside from tackling social issues and facing cultural/political confrontations, Khatami had to deal with major economic issues that needed urgent attention.

6.1 Political and Economic Developments

The IRI faced substantial economic problems when Khatami came to power in 1997. Global oil prices considerably declined and reduced foreign oil revenues; massive budget deficits and foreign debt caused rising inflation rates; the unemployment rate remained high amid a large and young population; and budgetary and legal constraints curtailed any significant structural changes or comprehensive reform plans during his initial years as president. The first two years of Khatami's presidency saw the continuation of the economic policies implemented by his predecessor Rafsanjani, mainly due to budgetary limitations caused by Iran's large foreign debt and opposition groups in the government. Also, because the *Majlis* was still dominated by conservatives in 1997, Khatami's administration faced considerable obstacles when addressing issues concerning social and political liberalization. Conservative hardliners repeatedly stressed the importance of improving the economy and dismissed social and political issues as "secondary and minor".[155] In response, Khatami identified the unequal distribution of capital, heavy dependence on oil exports, little sectoral output growth, high inflation and unemployment, budgetary deficits, excessive bureaucracy, and unfair business practices and regulations as the core economic problems plaguing the country. His proposition called for a greater role of the private sector, the attraction of foreign investment, the reduction of the state monopoly and the mobilization of domestic capital. His policies were much to the satisfaction of economic liberalists and the displeasure of the populist-statist faction, both of which had supported Khatami in his campaign for the presidency. In order to appease the conservatives, Khatami also purported to do his

---

[154] See: Siddiqi, Ahmad. „Khatami and the search for Reform in Iran," in *Stanford Journal of International Relations,* 2004.
http://www.stanford.edu/group/sjir/6.1.04_siddiqi.html

[155] In a 1999 speech to the *Majlis*, Khamenei reminded Khatami that "the most important problem of the country today…is the economic problem," which the president needed to pursue more seriously, rather than focusing on "secondary and minor issues."
See: Siddiqi, Ahmad. „Khatami and the search for Reform in Iran," in *Stanford Journal of International Relations,* 2004.
http://www.stanford.edu/group/sjir/6.1.04_siddiqi.html

best to uphold social Islamic justice (in other words, the status quo) and ensure an equitable distribution of capital among the population. Because of these conflicting policies, political restrictions, opposition from traditional conservatives, and limited government revenues, Khatami (during his first presidential term), was more or less forced to follow the course set out by the second Five Year Plan, which would last until 1999. On the 15th of September of the same year, the president presented his new Five Year Plan (2000-2005) to the *Majlis*, calling for economic reconstruction in a broader context of social and political development.

Once again, the country's heavy dependence on oil revenues proved to be a key factor in determining overall economic performance. An oil price shock in 1998, facilitated by a drop in world demand due to the Asian economic crisis of 1997, resulted in a -30% gross national product (GNP) of the oil sector. Consequently, many of Iran's chief economic sectors such as industry, manufacturing, and services posted significant declines in their average output. Reminiscent of the decline in sectoral output growth during the first Five Year Plan due to falling oil prices, the agricultural sector was one of the few sectors not detrimentally affected during the oil price shock and actually demonstrated an increase of nearly 20% GNP between 1997/98 and 1998/99. As oil prices stabilized the following year, GNP growth in the agricultural sector fell from 31.5% in 1998/99 to 25.3% in 1999/00, whereas alternative sectors again posted gains. In 1998, the national account balance registered at -$2.1 billion, the price of crude oil dipped below $10 a barrel in June, and the GDP per capita declined by nearly $200. The GDP per capita actually declined from $1745 in 1997 to $1582 in 1998. Because Khatami mostly followed the agenda of the second Five Year Plan during his first term, he did not manage to attain any significant changes or improvements economically. The lack of underutilized production capacities caused the economy to grow at a very slow pace despite a significant rise in oil prices after 1994. Political and macroeconomic instability and declining growth rates forced the government to postpone badly needed structural reforms.[156] Dismal economic conditions were characterized by:

- high inflation and unemployment rates,

[156] See: Valadkhani, A. "An Analysis of Iran's Third Five-Year Development Plan in the Post-Revolution Era (2000-2005)," in *Journal of Iranian Research and Analysis*, 2001, 17(2), p. 10. http://ro.uow.edu.au/commpapers/399

- the reduction in the national income from 18.4% in 1997/98 to 12.8% in 1998/99,
- widespread rent-seeking behavior,
- credit allocations for *bonyads* and state-owned enterprises,
- and extensive subsidies of petroleum products.

Table 10: Growth Rate of the Gross National Product by Kind of Economic Activity (1996-2001) (Percent, at current prices)

	1996/97	1997/98	1998/99	1999/00	2000/01
Agriculture	12,4	11,0	31,5	15,3	20,9
Oil and Gas	33,0	-2,5	-30,7	123,9	60,7
Industries and Mines	51,6	16,8	6,6	30,3	35,6
Mining	35,6	12,3	25,0	25,0	22,6
Manufacturing	47,4	23,7	7,0	29,8	34,0
Electricity, Gas and Water Supply	55,6	24,6	20,0	24,5	102,0
Construction	64,4	-1,0	0,2	34,6	26,5
Services	33,2	26,8	21,3	24,7	27,7
Trade, Restaurants and Hotels	35,7	16,8	23,5	24,0	21,1
Transportation, Warehousing and Communication	52,9	33,0	9,2	22,9	49,4
Financial Services	21,7	24,2	52,1	49,6	49,5
Real Estate and Professional Services	39,2	41,0	25,2	24,4	18,7
Public Services	17,9	22,5	19,3	22,3	29,9
Social, Personal and Domestic Services	32,0	22,0	23,5	35,7	29,2
Gross Domestic Product in Basic Prices	32,3	17,2	12,6	32,2	32,7
GDP in Basic prices (Except Oil)	32,2	21,2	19,6	23,6	27,9
Gross National Product (in Market Prices)	33,7	18,4	12,8	32,3	33,2
Less: Consumption of Fixed Capital	35,1	15,0	12,8	24,6	22,4
National Income	31,8	18,3	12,9	33,3	34,8

Source: Bank Markazi Jomhuri-ye Eslami-ye Iran. *Economic Report and Balance Sheet*, various issues.

Table 11: Selected Data on the Economy of the IRI (1997-2004)

Subject Description	Units	Scale	1997	1998	1999	2000	2001	2002	2003	2004
Current Account Balance	Billions	US Dollars	2.2	-2.1	6.5	12.5	5.9	3.5	0.8	3.9
Current Account Balance in % of GDP		Ratio	2.1	-2.2	6.3	13.0	5.2	3.1	0.6	2.5
GDP per capita, current prices		US Dollars	1745	1582	1665	1509	1776	1761	1989	2362
GDP, constant prices, annual % change		Percent	3.4	2.7	1.9	5.1	3.7	7.5	6.7	5.6
GDP, current prices	Billions	US Dollars	106.3	97.8	104.6	96.4	115.4	116.4	133.7	161.4
Inflation		Index 2000=100	62.6	73.9	88.8	100.0	111.4	129.0	149.1	171.7
Inflation, annual percentage change		Percent	17.3	18.1	20.1	12.6	11.4	15.8	15.6	15.2

Source: International Monetary Fund (IMF) *World Economic Outlook Database*, 2007.

During his first term as president, Khatami also attempted to relax the IRI's foreign policy stance by improving relations with states inside and outside the region. In 1997, then-president of the U.S. Bill Clinton saw an opportunity to capitalize on President Khatami's pro-reform and liberal stance to improve U.S.-Iran relations. In January 1998, Khatami addressed the American nation on CNN by stressing that Iran had "no hostility" towards them.[157] In 1999, steps toward rapprochement were taken by Clinton and Secretary of State Albright, both acknowledging that the IRI's antagonistic stance towards the U.S. and the West may have been justified in light of past grievances, including the CIA-engineered coup of democratically-elected Prime Minister Mossadegh in 1953 and U.S. military and financial support of Saddam Hussein during the Iran-Iraq war. The U.S. went so far as to ease economic sanctions on selected Iranian goods like pistachios, caviar, and carpets. However,

[157] BBC News. "Profile: Mohammad Khatami," June 30, 2003. http://news.bbc.co.uk/2/hi/middle_east/3027382.stm

whereas some reformists in the IRI perceived this gesture as early steps towards improved relations, the conservative camp remained sceptical. Ironically, because many of the ruling conservatives control extensive sectors of the economy, they actually stood to profit more from the ease of sanctions than the majority of the population.[158] Ultimately, past policy failures and considerable conservative pressure both in the U.S. and the IRI prevented both Clinton's and Khatami's efforts to normalize relations between the two countries.

The conservative opposition at home also made it very difficult for Khatami to implement his desired domestic reforms. In 1997, he had won the presidency on a platform that emphasized the rule of law and the ease of civil liberties. Politically, however, Khatami's desire for social reform was staunchly opposed by traditional conservatives. Intimidation tactics were employed by conservatives to dissuade unison among Khatami's administration, deter the forming of alliances, and limit the reformist movement. Khatami's reformist interior minister, Abdollah Noori, was impeached and imprisoned after only eleven months in office on grounds of insulting Islamic values. On March 12, 2000 a prominent reformist tactician and key ally of Khatami, Saeed Hajjarian, was permanently injured in a botched assassination attempt by a member of the *Basij* militia. Despite these events, the first years of Khatami's presidency did actually witness greater social freedoms (i.e. increase in satellite dishes, more relaxed attitude concerning women's attire, etc.), the rapid increase of reformist newspapers, the introduction of new measures to promote a freer press, and greater accessibility to information from abroad. Ahmad Siddiqi notes that "people were openly discussing issues, such as the role of the *faqih* and relations with the United States, which had long been considered taboo."[159] On July 7, 1999 conservative government officials, sensing a growing threat to their legitimacy and loss of social control, passed a bill in the *Majlis* to amend the 1985 Press Law.[160] "The amendments required newspaper publishers to submit the list of their employees to the judiciary, and journalists to reveal their sources, and empowered the Press Courts to overrule jury verdicts, conduct summary trials, and

[158] For instance, former President Rafsanjani is one of the leading pistachio vendors in the IRI.
[159] Siddiqi, Ahmad. „Khatami and the search for Reform in Iran," in *Stanford Journal of International Relations*. 2004.
http://www.stanford.edu/group/sjir/6.1.04_siddiqi.html
[160] The 1985 Iranian Press Law detailed the legal procedures for dealing with offenses by the press, defined to include all periodicals, including procedures to be followed in Press Courts.
See: Human Rights Watch. *The Iranian Legal Framework and International Law*. 1999.
http://www.hrw.org/reports/1999/iran/Iran99o-03.htm

pass on extremely serious cases to Revolutionary Courts dealing with accusations of treason and endangering national security."[161] These amendments resulted in the closure of a popular reformist newspaper, the *Salaam*. On July 8, 1999, President Khatami faced the first major domestic crisis of his tenure when several hundred Tehran University students held demonstrations to protest against the closure of the *Salaam*. They were attacked by vigilantes, with violent confrontations taking place in university dormitories.[162] Ultimately, news of the student protests spread to other parts of the country, triggering a wave of protests that culminated in six days of street riots in Tehran and other cities.[163] The *Basij* and *Ansar-e Hezbollah* units of the state along with the official law enforcement agencies were employed by the state to quell the riots, which had spread to other major cities like Isfahan, Shiraz, Mashad, Tabriz, and Yazd. By July 13, after several hundred arrests, the state's security and militia forces were able to restore stability. Supreme Leader Ayatollah Khamenei condemned the attack on the students and promised an official investigation, but, he also criticized them and argued that the riots were planned by opponents of the Islamic revolution and financed by the United States. By depicting the riots as a U.S. initiated effort to oust the Islamic system, conservative rulers in Tehran once again attempted to find a unifying enemy to bring Iranians together toward a single cause. Also, twenty-four commanders of the Revolutionary Guards, the internal security force of the Islamic Republic, issued a stern warning to Khatami, demanding immediate action.[164] The pressure and warnings coming from the conservative camp to take action posed a serious dilemma for Khatami. Because he was not willing to officially contradict the Supreme Leader, knowing that he had to work with Khamenei to realize his policy reforms, Khatami could not publicly support the student protestors. This illustrated the limitations and restraints of the Iranian president and Khatami's inability to achieve significant reforms without the consent of the conservative hardliners and theocrats in power. On July 14, 1999, in a display of political and religious unity, both the Supreme Leader and the President organized a

---

[161] Hiro, Dilip. *Iran Today*. London: Politico's Publishing, 2006, pp. 304-305.

[162] The *Ansar-e Hezbollah* refers to an Islamist, militant group whose ideology is devoted to the *velayat-e faqih*, Ayatollah, Khomeini's principles, and the eradication of foreign, non-Islamic influences. Along with the *Basij* force, they are said to "represent a key element of the Islamic Republic's hold on power" and are employed for the "violent repression" of social protests and dissident gatherings.
See: Molavi, Afshin. *The Soul of Iran*. B&T, 2001, pp.310-311.

[163] See: Siddiqi, Ahmad. „Khatami and the search for Reform in Iran," in *Stanford Journal of International Relations*, 2004.
http://www.stanford.edu/group/sjir/6.1.04_siddiqi.html

[164] Ibid.

popular parade of several hundred thousand people, with chants of "*Marg bar America!*" ("Death to America!") resounding in the streets in a show of support for the government. "Three weeks later, the fifty thousand strong *Basij* force in Tehran conducted the largest military maneuvers ever conducted. They carried out drills to break up demonstrations, staged mock commando raids and parachute drops."[165] This served as a stern reminder to the general public that the state had the necessary capability to quash future social dissent with force, if need be. As Dilip Hiro notes, the riots of July 1999 resulted in diminishing the students' power to shape the socio-political system, but it did not deter them from opposing the conservatives. If anything, it strengthened their resolve, which was highlighted in the February 2000 *Majlis* elections.

The parliamentary elections resulted in an overwhelming victory for pro-reform groups, who secured nearly 200 of the 290 *Majlis* seats, thus providing Khatami's desired policies of social and economic reform with added political leverage. His own sweeping re-election on June 6, 2001 paved the way for Iran's third Five Year Plan.[166] The proposed plan included:

- the promotion of key non-oil economic sectors such as agriculture and industry; enhanced economic growth
- the reduction of unemployment/ creation of more jobs (especially for the Iranian youth)
- budget and tax reforms; the stabilization of the national currency
- increased social egalitarianism through the implementation of responsible subsidies and controlled prices
- the continuation of privatization and the promotion of the private sector
- an increase in non-oil exports
- elimination of monopolies/promotion of greater competition
- improvement of educational services and the reduction of the gender-literacy gap

---

[165] Hiro, Dilip. *Iran Today*. London: Politico's Publishing, 2006, p.311.

[166] President Khatami won nearly four-fifths of the vote on a turnout of 67%, with his nearest rival only receiving 16% of the ballots.
See: Hiro, Dilip. *Iran Today*. London: Politico's Publishing, 2006, p. 181.

Specifically, it also planned to privatize several major industries, create 750,000 new jobs per year, achieve an average annual real GDP growth of 6% over the period, reduce subsidies for basic commodities, and undertake a wide range of fiscal and structural reforms.[167] Other objectives of the government included the floating of the rial and attracting $10 billion in oil, gas, and petrochemical investments.

But, Khatami's Five Year Plan placed greater focus on social justice and general prosperity, and less on economic growth and development. On August 24, 1999 Supreme Leader Khamenei delivered a speech to the Cabinet in which he reminded the President that "the most important problem of the country today…is the economic problem."[168] Hence, adjustments were made to the plan by the Assembly of Experts to put greater emphasis on economic development. However, major structural changes regarding privatization, the encouragement of foreign investment, and the reduced role of the public sector that were necessary for the long-term, positive development of the economy were not encouraged by the conservative factions in the government. The liberalization reforms of the 1990's and the negative social and economic impact it had on the state still weighed heavily on their minds. For instance, in 1999, the government made an attempt to privatize several major industries, including communications, post, rail, petrochemicals, and even upstream oil and gas. However these reform efforts were repeatedly thwarted by the conservative party, which supports monopolies, and those interest groups who enjoy an under-taxed economy.[169]

Initial economic developments of the third Five Year Plan were positive. The increase of oil prices from $10 a barrel in 1999 to $30 in 2000 was an unexpectedly positive turn of events for the government, because it had only projected an oil price rise of only $4 over the next year. What is more, oil production steadily increased amid soaring global oil prices from around 3.5 mb/d in 1998-2002 to over 4 mb/d from 2003 onwards.

---

167 Siddiqi, Ahmad. „Khatami and the search for Reform in Iran," in *Stanford Journal of International Relations,* 2004.
http://www.stanford.edu/group/sjir/6.1.04_siddiqi.html

168 Ibid.

169 Valadkhani, A. "An Analysis of Iran's Third Five-Year Development Plan in the Post-Revolution Era (2000-2005)," in *Journal of Iranian Research and Analysis*, 17(2), 2001, p. 16.
http://ro.uow.edu.au/commpapers/399

Table 12: Iranian Oil Production 1998-2006

Year	Oil Production (Thousand barrels daily)
1998	3855
1999	3603
2000	3818
2001	3794
2002	3543
2003	4183
2004	4248
2005	4268
2006	4343

Source: BP Statistical Review of World Energy Full Report 2007

This was a fortunate turn of events for the president, who was under enormous pressure to improve economic developments. It provided a significant boost in state profits and a support platform for Khatami's proposed government expenditure and investment programs. An Oil Stabilization Fund was set-up to deposit oil revenues above the budgeted amount. This was designed to negate extreme fluctuations in international oil prices, to promote exports and to create employment.[170] The discovery of new oil and gas fields also encouraged developments in private sectors of the economy. The growth rate of the GNP in the manufacturing sector increased from 7% in 1998/99 to 29.8% in 1999/00, and 34% in 2000/01. For instance, the car output was headed for one million in 2004, registering an elevenfold increase in a decade.[171] From 1999 to 2000, the national account balance nearly doubled from $6.5 billion to $12.5 billion, while the annual inflation percentage change was reduced from 20.1% to 12.6%. Annual percentage change in GDP showed an increase from 1.9% in 1999 to 5.1% in 2000. In 2003-2007, the IRI's export to import ratio measured in US dollars remained positive, although hydrocarbon exports constituted the majority of exports. A significant increase in foreign exchange reserves has also been a positive consequence of rising oil profits. The reserves nearly doubled from $24 billion in 2003 to $45 billion in 2005, with the trend continuing to climb.

[170] Valadkhani, A. "An Analysis of Iran's Third Five-Year Development Plan in the Post-Revolution Era (2000-2005)," in *Journal of Iranian Research and Analysis*, 17(2), 2001, p. 17. http://ro.uow.edu.au/commpapers/399

[171] Hiro, Dilip. *Iran Today*. London: Politico's Publishing, 2006. p. 206.

Table 13: Selected Data on the Economy of the IRI (2003-2004)

(a) Actual. (b) Economist Intelligence Unit estimates.	**2003(a)**	**2004(a)**
Real GDP growth (%)	7.1	5.1
Population (m)	68.0	68.7
Exports of goods fob (US$ million)	33,991.0	43,852.0
Imports of goods fob (US$ million)	29,561.0	38,199.0
Current-account balance (US$ million)	816.0	1,442.0
Foreign-exchange reserves excl gold (US$ million)	24,427.0	32,709.0
Total external debt (US$ billion)	12.3	13.6
Debt-service ratio, paid (%)	4.6(b)	4.1(b)
Exchange rate (av) IR:US$	8,193.9	8,614.0

Source: The Economist. *Country Briefings Iran: Economic Structure.* 2007. www.economist.com

However, as aforementioned, higher GDP growth rates and positive indicators resulting from increased oil profits do not necessarily reflect positive domestic developments. One of Khatami's top priorities during his tenure was the creation of new jobs. While he did manage to reduce the unemployment rate from 25% in 1999 to 15.7% in 2002, Khatami did not meet the target of creating 750,000 new jobs a year proposed in his Five Year Plan.

Figure 5: IRI Unemployment Rate (%) (1999-2007)

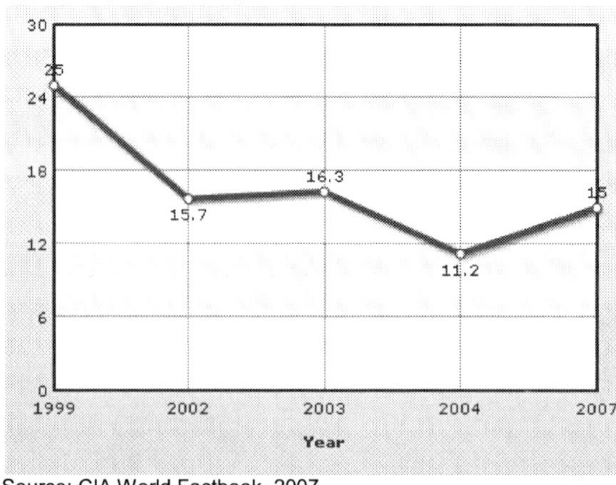

Source: CIA World Factbook. 2007.

This can be attributed to several factors. During the 1980's, political and religious leaders encouraged population growth that caused a population boom. The baby-boom generation, in turn, created a surplus of job-seekers that flooded the market. Consequently, the inadequate rate of economic growth could not keep pace with the rapid population growth. According to Jahangir Amuzegar, Iran's GDP must grow at a rate of at least 8% a year in real terms in order to absorb all the new job seekers, and by 9.5% to reduce unemployment below 10%. The Iranian economy's 5.4% average yearly growth between 1999 and 2003, however, was not adequate enough to generate needed outlets for all the new entrants. This led to the demand for new labor that lagged behind its supply by 30%.[172] Also, because the majority of the national economy is under state control, the bulk of government revenues accrued from external oil rents are reserved for public sector investments. Indicative of a rentier state, most heavy investments in the IRI are made in large, capital-intensive industries such as nuclear, hydrocarbons, base metals, and the military. "Directly resulting from this investment bias has been the low labor intensity of growth. According to an IMF report, while Iran's annual output growth has been comparable to the performance of "peer" countries in Asia, Africa, and Latin America, its employment elasticity (i.e. change in employment as a percentage of the labor force with respect to change in real non-oil GDP) has been relatively low."[173] Overburdened state-enterprises and institutions also can no longer accommodate the vast amount of job-seekers in the economy. Because some of the largest sectors in the IRI's economy, barring the hydrocarbon sector, are non-productive (i.e. services, government posts, etc.), the state has actually posted financial losses at the expense of maintaining them. By 2003, the amount of government employees had increased nearly sixfold since 1979, largely because of the incentives the IRI offered its' public servants. This, in turn, has caused many students to select opportunistic fields of study that will later provide them with access to patronage networks, instead of those that will provide them with the skills necessary for sustained economic development. For instance, Amuzegar notes that Iran's university graduates in humanities and Islamic studies outpace those in social sciences, commerce, and business

---

[172] See: Amuzegar, Jahangir. "Iran's Unemployment Crisis," in *Middle East Economic Survey*, vol. 47, no. 41, 2004.
http://www.mees.com/postedarticles/oped/a47n41d01.htm

[173] Amuzegar, Jahangir. "Iran's Unemployment Crisis," in *Middle East Economic Survey*, vol. 47, no. 41, 2004.
http://www.mees.com/postedarticles/oped/a47n41d01.htm

administration by a factor of 4 to 1.[174] Still, the decline in annual population growth is predicted to reduce the pressure on the job market in the coming decade, as long as economic growth can be consistently maintained or improved. In light of projected rises in the global price of crude, the IRI should be able to expand economic growth (at least over the next decade) and maintain its extensive public sector with windfall oil profits.

Politically, Khatami was determined to carry on his social liberalization reforms, despite staunch political opposition from the conservatives. During much of his presidential term, Khatami suffered numerous political setbacks concerning his social reform efforts. Many of his legislative bills that passed through the *Majlis* were eventually rejected by conservative hardliners in the Guardian Council. In 2002, he presented a set of "twin bills" to the *Majlis,* designed to expand the executive powers of the presidency. The first bill would enable him to prevent and reverse actions by the judiciary that violated the constitution. The second would bestow the president with the power to restrain the powers of the Council of Guardians by limiting its right to scrutinize and bar political candidates. Although both bills were adopted by the *Majlis*, it seemed highly unlikely that they would be approved by either the Guardian or Expediency Councils. The Guardian Council opted to prolong the ratification of the bills, instead of rejecting them outright, perhaps as a precautionary measure to prevent social and political turbulences. However, major social protests in November 2003, triggered by the sentencing of history professor Hashem Aghajari to death by the judiciary for allegedly insulting Islamic principles, could not be prevented by any faction in the state. This shifted the focus from Khatami's reform efforts to the restoration of social order. The mass protests of November 2003 were as serious and widespread as the student riots of 1999 and lasted for approximately an entire month; they eventually died down only after the judiciary repealed its death sentence of professor Aghajari and Khamenei's threat to use the *Basij* force to subdue dissidents.[175] By the time social order was restored, Khatami's reform movement had lost a lot of momentum, which enabled the Guardian Council to ultimately reject the twin bills without having to risk another societal backlash. In frustration, Khatami raised the prospect of resignation and boycotting the upcoming 2004 *Majlis* elections

[174] See: Amuzegar, Jahangir. "Iran's Unemployment Crisis," in *Middle East Economic Survey*, vol. 47, no. 41, 2004.
http://www.mees.com/postedarticles/oped/a47n41d01.htm

[175] Professor Aghajari's sentence was later reduced to three years in jail, two years of probation, and five years' suspension of his social rights. He was eventually released in 2004.

in light of his inability to implement the social reform programs which he had set out to do. But, considering the recent delicate state of the country, Khatami chose not to boycott the elections and later stated that “either we had to hold the elections or face riots."[176] Overall, President Khatami did not achieve the ambitious economic goals laid out in his third Five Year Plan partly because he devoted greater attention to attaining social reforms. Yet, his attempts to both implement pertinent social reforms and liberalize the economy were repeatedly thwarted by the clerical establishment, highlighting the limits of the presidency. Khatami's bold efforts to push for reforms resulted in a conservative backlash in the *Majlis* elections of 2004 and the presidential elections of 2005.

---

[176] China Daily. “Khatami: Iran's democratic reforms failed.” 2004. http://www.chinadaily.com.cn/english/doc/2004-12/07/content_397866.htm

7. PHASE IV: 2005-2008, CONSERVATIVE BACKLASH

Economic, political and social liberalization over the past decade and a half had increasingly empowered civil society and caused a drastic rise in the number of domestic protests and demonstrations directed against the government. This prompted a conservative backlash in the *Majlis* elections of 2004, during which the Guardian Council decided to disqualify 3,600 (mostly reformist) candidates out of 8,157 from running. Consequently, in February, the elections witnessed the conservatives' return to power amid boycotts from several reformist parties protesting the disqualification of their candidates. "The loss of the reformists can be attributed as much to the mass disqualification of their candidates and the subsequent boycotts, as to voter apathy."[177] Having experienced repeated failures by the reformists to achieve any meaningful social, political and cultural freedoms, the electorate chose to place greater emphasis on economic issues. This proved to be advantageous for the next conservative candidate who would eventually win the presidential elections of 2005. Mahmoud Ahmadinejad, a former mayor of Tehran, ran his presidential candidacy on a populist platform of fighting corruption, aiding the poor, maintaining food and fuel subsidies, providing interest-free loans to farmers and small businesses and redistributing the country's oil wealth to the needy. His main rival, the former pragmatic president Rafsanjani, attempted to re-brand himself as a reformist and promised to pursue a policy of "meaningful" reforms that would see the continuation of his former policies of political and economic liberalization.[178] However, both reformists like Khatami and pragmatic conservatives like Rafsanjani had overlooked the neglected issues of the poor and urban class workers. Their policies of social and economic reforms had appealed to the middle and upper classes of society, virtually ignoring the economic hardships that an ever-increasing number of Iranians had to endure. Ahmadinejad, on the other hand, approached a bottom-up strategy of mixing socially with working and lower-class Iranians.[179] On August 6, 2005, Mahmoud Ahmadinejad became the sixth president of the IRI after garnering 62% of 29 million votes in the run-off poll.

---

[177] Siddiqi, Ahmad. „Khatami and the search for Reform in Iran," in *Stanford Journal of International Relations,* 2004.
http://www.stanford.edu/group/sjir/6.1.04_siddiqi.html

[178] See: Hiro, Dilip. *Iran Today*. London: Politico's Publishing, 2006, p. 373.

[179] Ibid.

7.1 Political and Economic Developments

Ahmadinejad's assumption of the presidency and the domination of the *Majlis* by the conservatives shifted the center of political power to the right in "religious-ideological terms and left in the economic sphere, reflecting primarily the values of the emergent urban working class--economically leftist but religiously and socially conservative."[180] Having publicly expressed his loyalty to Tehran's conservative clerical establishment by symbolically kissing Supreme Leader Khamenei's hand during the presidential inauguration, Ahmadinejad clearly signalled his intention to pursue more protectionist and conservative economic and political policies.

As of 2005, the Iranian economy still had to deal with high inflation rates hovering around 16%, unemployment rates (officially) at 25%, weak output growth in essential non-oil sectors like industry and manufacturing, and an economic environment not conducive to foreign direct investment. However, perhaps the single and most important economic factor for the Iranian rentier state, namely oil, posted dramatic global price increases. Although projected oil revenues for the IRI in 2005 were estimated to be around $16 billion, they exceeded $35 billion by the end of the year as a result of the price hike, even with daily oil production remaining constant at 4.2 mb/d. The average yearly price of crude soared from just under $40 a barrel in 2004 to nearly $100 a barrel by the end of 2007. Consequently, this also increased the non-gold foreign-exchange reserves from $32 billion in 2004 to over $64 billion in 2007. Real GDP has remained constant at around 4.5% between 2005 and 2007 and the GDP per capita increased from $2425 to $4013.

Table 14: Selected Data on the Economy of the I.R. of Iran (2005-2007)

Subject Description	**Units**	**Scale**	**2005**	**2006**	**2007**
Current Account Balance	Billions	US Dollars	14.7	18.1	18.0
Current Account Balance in % of GDP		Ratio	7.5	7.6	6.2
GDP per capita,		US Dollars	2825	3400	4013

180 Hiro, Dilip. *Iran Today*. London: Politico's Publishing, 2006, p. 376.

current prices					
GDP, constant prices, annual % change		Percent	5.9	5.3	5.0
GDP, current prices	Billions	US Dollars	196.4	240.4	288.5
Inflation		Index 2000=100	194.1	227.1	265.7
Inflation, annual percentage change		Percent	13.0	17.0	17.0

Source: International Monetary Fund (IMF) *World Economic Outlook Database*, 2007.

Table 15: Selected Data on the Economy of the IRI (2005-2007)

(a) Actual. (b) Economist Intelligence Unit estimates.	**2005(a)**	**2006(b)**	**2007(b)**
Real GDP growth (%)	4.4	4.3	4.3
Population (m)	69.4	70.3(a)	70.9
Exports of goods fob (US$ million)	60,012.0	66,797.1	71,447.8
Imports of goods fob (US$ million)	40,969.0	45,667.4	48,064.9
Current-account balance (US$ million)	14,037.0	16,657.8	18,999.4
Foreign-exchange reserves excl gold (US$ million)	45,209.0(b)	58,209.0	64,209.0
Total external debt (US$ billion)	13.9	13.7	13.8
Debt-service ratio, paid (%)	3.6(b)	2.9	2.6
Exchange rate (av) IR:US$	8,964.0	9,170.9(a)	9,407.5

Source: The Economist. *Country Briefings Iran: Economic Structure,* 2007. www.economist.com

Yet, President Ahmadinejad's campaign promises of alleviating poverty, creating jobs, fighting corruption and improving the economy have not been realized so far, which can be traced to the refusal of the conservative rulers in Tehran to undertake comprehensive and meaningful economic reforms in order to maintain their hold on power at the expense of the general population. Poverty levels remain high while the gap between the wealthy and the poor has widened. The lack of an efficient tax collection system has made it difficult for Ahmadinejad to reduce this gap, because minimal tax revenues have forced him to use oil rents to cover the IRI's national budget. The absence of crucial financial information about citizens, which a functioning tax system would have provided the government with, has made it that much more difficult for the state to effectively and equitably redistribute oil wealth to those who need it the most. Also, inefficient financial regulations and the lack of transparency have provided large sections of the economy like the *bonyads*, which are unaccountable to government oversight and exempt from taxes, with the opportunity to amass vast financial resources. *Bonyads* have served as an ideal venue for corrupt officials and patronage networks, and have virtually been transformed into private monopolies that crowd out smaller private companies and are detrimental to fair economic competition. The Iranian *bazaar*, another key sector of the economy, has also managed to circumvent lax government regulations and taxation, yearly costing the IRI millions in lost tax revenues. As oil profits have increased drastically over the past decade, so has government spending. The IRI's government expenditure before 2002 averaged at about $15 billion in foreign exchange. In three years, this figure increased to $36 billion in 2005, an indication of the state's heavy budgetary dependence on external oil rents. Also, despite a positive export to import ratio (the ratio is positive chiefly due to its vast hydrocarbon exports), the IRI's import of foreign goods has posted a consistent increase from $40 billion in 2005 to $48 billion in 2007. This, in turn, has had a damaging effect on Iran's non-oil economic sectors, hinting at the effects of Dutch Disease. As a result, instead of reducing its dependence on oil revenues, the IRI has increasingly become more dependent on it because of the higher demand of foreign imports and the need to compensate for and maintain economic sectors with weak output growths. Furthermore, the considerable inflow of foreign currency into the economy has induced lavish domestic spending and capital-intensive investments in construction and nuclear projects (while neglecting other key sectors) that have made it difficult for Ahmadinejad's administration to combat inflation. The state continues to heavily subsidize food and gasoline, burdening its own national budget in the process. Additionally, the lack of refineries in the hydrocarbon sector due to poor infrastructure and investment has forced the government to import gasoline to meet rising domestic demands. Overall, the IRI suffered from high unemployment and inflation rates, inefficient tax and information extraction capacities, state-run monopolies and charitable foundations, corruption, and an environment not conducive to foreign direct investment long before the current president's election in 2005. Mahmoud Ahmadinejad's economic policies, a reflection of the conservative agenda of hardliners in Tehran, have only served to exacerbate the economic situation further. The government is well aware of the reforms it would have to undertake to attain long-term economic prosperity. The reduction of state subsidies, privatization, increased transparency and accountability, improved wealth distribution, an efficient tax and information extraction system, and the establishment of an economic environment favorable to foreign direct investment are but to name a few. However, traditional conservatives have good reason to resist the implementation of such policies. The economic and social reforms of President Rafsanjani and President Khatami in the 1990's and the early 2000's demonstrated the risks for the state of permitting such liberalization measures, while attempting to maintain firm social and political control. The currency crisis of the mid-1990's, increasing popular dissent (even among the traditional power base of conservatives), the major student riots of 1999 and mass protests in 2003 during the liberalization periods served as warning signals for Tehran's conservative ruling elite.

President Ahmadinejad's firm stance against economic and political liberalization measures hints at the IRI's shift to a more assertive foreign policy as well as the reinforcement of authoritarian control domestically. He has adopted a critical position towards the U.S., Israel, and the West and pursued an ambitious nuclear program, asserting the IRI's right to develop peaceful nuclear energy. Due to the military quagmire of the U.S. in Iraq and Afghanistan, Western powers have attempted to curb Iran's rising influence in the Middle East through international sanctions and diplomatic efforts, realizing that military action is not a viable option at the moment. However, this has proven to be minimally effective thus far. With global oil prices reaching record highs of over $120 a barrel in 2008, Iran's vast hydrocarbon reserves have become more valuable and provide it with added financial and political leverage. The IRI is increasingly aware of its geopolitical and geo-economic importance and knows how to utilize it against its foreign rivals. For the time being (and likely, over the next few years if global crude prices register a consistent upward trend), windfall oil profits will enable the state to ride out economic periods of difficulty and minimize the effects of international economic sanctions and isolation policies. In fact, international isolation is welcomed by hardliner conservatives, whose experiences over the past 30 years have illustrated that it has actually reinforced their internal consolidation of authoritarian power. By alienating the U.S. and the West, Ahmadinejad seeks to increase the country's international isolation while reducing destabilizing external factors such as foreign products, media, etc. that could potentially enter Iran. In reducing the permeability of Iran's borders to foreign influence, ruling elites hope to increase the population's dependency on the state. Because the IRI is based on a rentier system, increased dependency of the populace will effectively strengthen state institutions and parastatal foundations like the *bonyads,* which serve as mechanisms for wealth distribution.

The foreign policy pursued by President George W. Bush after the Sept. 11, 2001 terrorist attacks on the World Trade Centers has contributed to the exacerbation of relations between the IRI and the U.S. During his State of the Union Address in 2002, President Bush included Iran, Iraq, and North Korea as part of the "axis of evil", a term used to describe governments supporting international terrorism and seeking weapons of mass destruction. To combat global terrorism, the U.S. subsequently initiated its' "War on Terror" campaign, which conducted pre-emptive wars in Afghanistan in 2001 and Iraq in 2003. The resulting military occupation of two of Iran's neighboring countries worried conservatives in Tehran and prompted them to vigorously pursue the development of nuclear technology. John Mearsheimer, a professor at the University of Chicago, claims that "the country that acquires nuclear weapons becomes unattackable...it is precisely for that reason that it wants them."[181] Although repeatedly stressing the IRI's right to acquire nuclear technology, Mahmoud Ahmadinejad has had difficulties in convincing the international community of Iran's peaceful intentions, especially after his controversial and provocative remarks regarding Israel.[182] Nevertheless, U.S. and European efforts to halt Iran's uranium enrichment program through the United Nations Security Council and the International Atomic Energy Agency (IAEA) have proven to be ineffective. Both Russia and China have repeatedly opposed initiatives to impose stricter sanctions on

[181] Cited from: Hiro, Dilip. *Iran Today*. London: Politico's Publishing, 2006, p.386.

[182] President Ahmadinejad has called for Israel to be "wiped off the map" and described the Holocaust as a "myth".

the IRI and President Ahmadinejad enjoys broad-based domestic support for the nuclear program, especially because of the threat of a possible military strike by the U.S. or Israel. With U.S. armed forces heavily pre-occupied in Iraq and Afghanistan and global oil prices soaring, Iran's conservatives have opted to maintain their confrontational stance towards the West. By alienating the U.S. and Europe, the IRI seeks to increase its' international isolation, which would strengthen the government's position internally by increasing the populace's dependence on the state. It can afford to isolate itself because recent windfall oil profits have provided Iran with the necessary capital to sustain its domestic economy and state structures. In light of record oil prices exceeding $120 a barrel in 2008, the threat of an oil embargo by the international community to put pressure on the state also seems unlikely. The impact of such an embargo would prove to be more harmful to major oil-importing countries like the U.S. and Europe. In contrast to the U.S.'s uncompromising policy on Iran, the easing of international sanctions and the encouragement of economic and social liberalization would likely prove to be more effective in weakening Iran's authoritarian government than military threats and economic embargoes.

8. CONCLUSION

Benjamin Smith states that the central principle of democratic transition studies is that authoritarian regimes are more likely to collapse during times of economic crises or shocks.[183] The logic behind this line of reasoning is that "economic crises undercut a regime's political legitimacy, creating a groundswell of dissent that may catalyze authoritarian breakdown. Thus, those economic crises that evolve into political ones hold the potential for regime change."[184] Yet, the IRI, being a major global oil-exporter and external rent-dependent state which has been very susceptible to the extreme price volatility of global oil prices and economic shocks of the past 30 years, has demonstrated strong persistence and durability. As outlined in the previous chapters, it survived difficult periods of political turmoil, economic crises, war, international sanctions and isolation while it relied on oil profits as its primary source of income. Because oil proceeds comprise the bulk of state revenues, the IRI's government has not deemed it necessary to expand its extractive capacities,

[183] Smith, Benjamin. "The Wrong Kind of Crisis: Why Oil Booms and Busts Rarely Lead to Authoritarian Breakdown," in *Studies in Comparative International Development*, Winter 2006, vol. 40, no. 4, p. 55.
[184] Ibid.

especially during boom cycles. Instead, government activity has been primarily concerned with the political redistribution of rent through patronage networks in order to "purchase" political consensus and reduce pressures for representation and accountability.[185] According to rentier theory, a state's weak or lacking extractive capacities may hinder "the kinds of iterated and multifaceted interactions between rulers and ruled that provide both public participation in policymaking and a means by which rulers keep an eye on the public."[186] This should produce weak state-society linkages and instability "both during booms, when politicians are likely to flood the domestic economy with revenues, spending unwisely and spurring destabilizing inflation, and busts, when weak state institutions prove unable to continue patronage and extract revenues from domestic sources." [187] Although the IRI has experienced periods of instability, the causal factors had less to do with weak state-society linkages than with alternative causes.

In the first chapter, I provided three factors that contribute to regime durability in the IRI, namely: international isolation, external threats, and a rentier system. However, a rentier system can only be a contributing factor to regime stability if two important preconditions can been met, namely sustained (but not necessarily consistent) external oil rents and the presence of strong, pre-existing state structures, established after a robust coalition- and institution-building process. Benjamin Smith has stressed that the *timing* of the onset of oil-profits and wealth allocation is crucial. He argues that "oil wealth tends to produce...two political trajectories, depending on its timing relative to "late" development and to the strength of opposition to rulers at the onset of late development. One trajectory results in weak regimes commanding weak institutions. In the other trajectory, oil wealth facilitates building robust regime coalitions and powerful institutions, enabling rulers to ride out oil-induced crises that undercut other governments."[188] The timing of the onset of oil wealth in the IRI was crucial to its subsequent economic and political development. "Late development" is defined as a set of policies in which "the state explicitly nurtures the development of private sector capital and labor, relying on a variety of means-financial, social,

---

185 Karl, Terry. "Oil-led Development: Social, Political, and Economic Consequences," in *CDDRL Working Papers.* Stanford University. 2007, p.21. http://cddrl.stanford.edu/publications/oilled_development_social_political_and_economic_consequences/

186 Smith, Benjamin. *Hard Times in the Lands of Plenty: Oil Politics in Iran and Indonesia.* Ithaca, NY: Cornell University Press. 2007, p.17.

187 Ibid., p.18.

188 Smith, Benjamin. "The Wrong Kind of Crisis: Why Oil Booms and Busts Rarely Lead to Authoritarian Breakdown," in *Studies in Comparative International Development*, Winter 2006, vol. 40, no. 4, p. 56.

political, and infrastructural"[189] and/or "more directly interventionist policies such as the creation of state-owned industrial enterprises and state-granted monopolies in key sectors."[190] The latter argument applies to the IRI.

Directly after the Islamic revolution of 1979, Khomeini and his supporters experienced a difficult period of post-revolutionary turmoil, international isolation, and external threats. This combination of factors had several related effects. The international isolation of Iran as a consequence of the revolution, the U.S. hostage crisis and the financial burden of an eight-year war with Iraq consequently decreased the state's oil revenues. Because Khomeini's government initially did not have access to sufficient capital to "purchase" the loyalty of opposition and dissident groups, it was forced to make a number of concessions, co-opt and form coalitions in order to remain in power. The nationalization of key enterprises like the NIOC and the creation of state-granted monopolies like the *bonyads* provided a foundation for strong state and semi-state structures which would later serve as mechanisms for rent redistribution and the consolidation of regime power. Meanwhile, the presence of external threats (Iran-Iraq war) aided in maintaining internal cohesion while providing the state and its institutions legitimacy. Thus, after successfully establishing strong state structures and forming robust coalitions, the IRI utilized its rentier system to reinforce its' extensive state-owned enterprises and economic sectors. Being the ultimate driver of the economy because of its exclusive access to external oil rents, the IRI increased the public's dependency on the state through patronage networks, its vast control of the public sector and state subsidies. This system has acted as a support structure during times of economic and political hardships, which have usually been induced during periods of liberalization and reforms in the absence of significant external threats. The more the IRI pursued liberalization, privatization, and social and economic reform policies, the more internal difficulties did it face, as was the case during both Rafsanjani and Khatami's presidencies. Without the unifying effect of an external threat and decreased international isolation, Iran was exposed to the effects of globalization and foreign influence which increased domestic dissidence in light of economic and social problems. Only strong state and semi-state structures that have been maintained by the IRI's rentier system including the

[189] Bellin,Eva. *Stalled Democracy: Capital, Labor, and the Paradox of State-Sponsored Development.* Ithaca: Cornell University. 2002, pp. 3-4.

[190] Smith, Benjamin. *Hard Times in the Lands of Plenty: Oil Politics in Iran and Indonesia.* Ithaca, NY: Cornell University Press. 2007, p.3.

bonyads, state-owned corporations, the *Basij*, and the Revolutionary Guards, among others, possessed the necessary capacity to suppress internal unrest or appease the masses. It is important to note the interdependency of the stabilizing factors. Increased international isolation strengthens the rentier system of the IRI, because it increases domestic dependency on the state. During oil busts, Iran's rentier system may weaken, but the government can still utilize the two other factors to reinforce its position, which was precisely the case during the Iran-Iraq war. Currently, Mahmoud Ahmadinejad's administration, even amid soaring global oil prices, has been experiencing increased social unrest and opposition due to his failed economic programs. Therefore, he has actively pursued a hardline, conservative foreign policy in order to increase Iran's international isolation as well as to draw threats from the U.S. and Israel to unify the domestic population against a common cause and deflect their attention away from internal economic and social problems. If the rising global demand for oil and gas and the increasingly confrontational Iranian nuclear issue is an indication, the theocratic government in Tehran for the conceivable future can only be strengthened in light of the international community's short-sighted policy of isolation and containment.

Table 16: Phases of Increased Authoritarian Stability/Instability in the IRI

Phases	Stabilizing Factors	Destabilizing Factors	Increasing/Decreasing Stability
Phase I (1979-1988)	-Iran-Iraq War -International sanctions -Rentier system -Coalition-building -Establishment of strong institutions, state and parastatal structures	-Initial political turmoil	Overall increased authoritarian stability (Consolidation of power; coalition-building; common enemy; international isolation, etc.)
Phase II (1989-1997)	-Strong state and parastatal structures (i.e. *bonyads*, *Basij*, Revolutionary Guards, etc.) -Rentier System (Maintained state security during periods of social unrest by providing reinforcement for state apparatuses)	-Economic liberalization -Lack of significant external threats -Decreased international isolation	Overall decreased authoritarian stability (Lack of unifying, external threat; opening of domestic markets, etc.)
Phase III (1997-2004)	See above.	-Social and economic liberalization (Civil liberties, increased freedom of expression, etc.) -Increased accessibility to international markets	Overall decreased authoritarian stability (Domestic unrest; increased social and economic demands)
Phase IV (2005-Present)	-Increased international isolation -Newly imposed sanctions -Nuclear issue -Retraction of social and economic liberalization measures	-Inefficient rent distribution -Economic difficulties	Overall increased authoritarian stability (Presence of a unifying external enemy i.e. U.S., Israel, Europe; increased dependence of society on the state due to greater isolation and sanctions; consolidation of social control.)

BIBLIOGRAPHY

Abrahamian, Ervand. 1982. *Iran Between Two Revolutions*. Princeton: Princeton University Press.

Afrasiabi, K.1994. *After Khomeini. New Directions in Iran's Foreign Policy.* San Francisco and Oxford.

Alizadeh, Parvin. 2000. *"The Economy of Iran: Dilemmas of an Islamic State."* London and New York, I.B. Tauris.

Amirahamdi, Hooshang.1990. *Revolution and Economic Transition: The Iranian Experience.* Albany: State University of New York Press.

Amirahmadi, Hooshang. March, 18, 1996.*Iran's Power Structure.* http://www.iranian.com/Mar96/Opinion/AmirIran.html

Amuzegar, Jahangir. 1993. *Iran's Economy Under the Islamic Republic*. New York and London: I. B. Tauris.

Amuzegar, Jahangir. 2004. "Iran's Unemployment Crisis," in *Middle East Economic Survey*, vol. 47, no. 41. http://www.mees.com/postedarticles/oped/a47n41d01.htm

Associated Press. Dec. 26, 2006. "Iran Revenue Quickly Drying Up, Analysis Says," in *Washington Post.* http://www.washingtonpost.com/wpdyn/content/article/2006/12/25/AR2006122500486.html

Atieh Bahar. 2002. *Iran Country Profile & Business Guide Geography, Population & Climate.* www.atiehbahar.com

Auty, R. 2001. *Resource Abundance and Economic Development*. Oxford: Oxford University Press.

Bahrmabeygui, H. 1977. *Tehran: An Urban Analysis.* Tehran: Sahab Books Institute.

Bakhash, Shaul. 1990. *The Reign of the Ayatollahs: Iran and the Islamic Revolution.* New York: Basic Books.

Baland, J.-M. and P. Francois. 2000. "Rent-seeking and resource booms," in *Journal of Development Economics* vol.61, p.527-542.

Bank Markazi Jomhuri-ye Eslami-ye Iran. *Economic Report and Balance Sheet*, various issues.

Bank Markazi Jomhuri-ye Eslami-ye Iran. 1981. *Hesabha-ye Melli-ye Iran 1338-1356 (1959/60-1977/78)*.Tehran.

Bank Markazi Jomhuri-ye Eslami-ye Iran. 1991. *Hesabha-ye Melli-ye Iran 1353-1366 (1974/75-1987/88)*.Tehran.

Bank Markazi Jomhuri-ye Eslami-ye Iran. 1978/79 to 1990/91. *Gozaresh-e Eqtesadi va Taraznameh.* Tehran.

Bank Markazi Jomhuri-ye Eslami-ye Iran. 1984? *Barrasi-e Tahavolat-ye Keshvar baad az Enqelab.* Tehran.

Baran, P. 1973. *The Political Economy of Growth*. Harmondsworth: Penguin.

Barkey, Henri J. 1992 (ed.). *The Politics of Economic Reform in the Middle East.* New York: St. Martin's Press.

Bayat, Assef. 1987. *Workers and Revolution in Iran*. London: Zed Press.

BBC News. "Profile: Mohammad Khatami," June 30, 2003. http://news.bbc.co.uk/2/hi/middle_east/3027382.stm

BBC News. 2008. "In Depth: Iran, Who Holds the Power?" http://news.bbc.co.uk/2/shared/spl/hi/middle_east/03/iran_power/html/default.stm

Beblawi, Hazem and Giacomo Luciani, eds. 1987. *The Rentier State.* London, New York, Sydney: Croom Helm.

Beblawi, Hazem.1990. "The Rentier State in the Arab World," in Giacomo Luciani (ed.), *The Arab State.* London.

Beck, Martin and Oliver Schlumberger.1998. "Der Vordere Orient – ein entwicklungs-politischer Sonderfall?" In: *Der Bürger im Staat,* vol. 48/3.

Bellin,Eva. 2002. *Stalled Democracy: Capital, Labor, and the Paradox of State-Sponsored Development.* Ithaca: Cornell University.

Bill, James A. and Robert Springborg.1994. *Politics in the Middle East.* New York: Harper Collins.

Bostock, Frances and Geoffrey Jones. 1989. *Planning and Power in Iran: Ebtehaj and Economic Development under the Shah.* London: Frank Cass.

BP Statistical Review of World Energy Full Report 2007 http://www.bp.com/liveassets/bp_internet/globalbp/globalbp_uk_english/reports_and_publications/statistical_energy_review_2007/STAGING/local_assets/downloads/pdf/statistical_review_of_world_energy_full_report_2007.pdf

Brown, Nathan. 1997. "Sharia and State in the Modern Muslim Middle East" in *International Journal of Middle East Studies*, no.29, pp. 359-376.

Brumberg, Daniel. 2001. *Reinventing Khomeini: The Struggle for Reform in Iran.* Chicago and London: University of Chicago Press.

Brumberg, Daniel and Ariel Ahram. 2007. *The National Iranian Oil Company in Iranian Politics.* The James A. Baker III Institute for Public Policy, Rice University.

Buchta, Wilfried. 2000. *Who Rules Iran? The Structure of Power in the Islamic Republic.* Washington D.C.: The Washington Institute for Near East Policy.

Cardoso, Fernando Henrique and Enzo Faletto. 1978. *Dependency and Development in Latin America.* Berkeley: University of California Press.

China Daily. 2004. "Khatami: Iran's democratic reforms failed." http://www.chinadaily.com.cn/english/doc/2004-12/07/content_397866.htm

Choudhuri, M.A. and U.A. Malik. 1992. *The Foundations of Islamic Political Economy.* London: Macmillan.

CIA World Factbook. May 2008. https://www.cia.gov/library/publications/the-world-factbook/geos/ir.html

Clark, John F. 2005. "Petroleum Revenues and Political Development in the Congo Republic: The Democratic Experiment and Beyond," in *Basedau/Mehler (eds.) (2005): Resource Politics in sub-Saharan Africa.* Hamburg: Hamburg African Studies No. 13.

Colville, Thierry (ed.). 1994. *The Economy of Islamic Iran: Between State and Market.* Louvain: Peeters for Institut Francais de Recherché en Iran.

Contreras, Ricardo. March 25, 2008. "Competing Theories of Economic Development." http://www.uiowa.edu/ifdebook/ebook2/contents/part1-III.shtml

Corden, W. M. 1984. "Booming Sector and Dutch Disease Economics: Survey and Consolidation," in *Oxford Economic Papers*, vol. 36, no. 3.

Dasgupta, P.S. and G.M. Heal. 1979. *Economic Theory and Exhaustible Resources.* Cambridge: Cambridge University Press.

Ehteshami, Anoushirvan. 1995. *After Khomeini: The Second Iranian Republic.* London and New York: Routledge.

Eickelman, Dale E. and James Piscator. 1996. *Muslim Politics.* Princeton: Princeton University Press.

Elm, Mostafa. 1992. *Oil, Power, and Principle: Iran's Oil Nationalization and its Aftermath.* Syracuse: Syracuse University Press.

Elsenhans, Hartmut.1981. *Abhängiger Kapitalismus oder bürokratische Entwicklungsgesellschaft. Essays über den Staat in der heutigen Dritten Welt.* Frankfurt am Main: Campus Verlag.

Energy Information Administration (EIA)
http://www.eia.doe.gov/emeu/cabs/AOMC/Overview.html

Esposito, John. 1992. *The Islamic Threat: Myth or Reality?* New York: Oxford University Press.

Evans, Peter. 1979. *Dependent Development: The Alliance of Multinational, State, and Local Capital in Brazil.* Princeton: Princeton University Press.

Evans, Peter, Dietrich Rueschermeyer, and Theda Skocpol, eds.1985. *Bringing the State Back In.* Cambridge: Cambridge University Press.

Farhi, Farideh. 1990. *States and Urban-Based Revolutions: Iran and Nicaragua.* Chicago: University of Illinois Press.

Fesharaki, Fereidun.1985. "Iran's Petroleum Policy: How does the Oil Industry Function in Revolutionary Iran?" in Afshar, H. (ed.), *A Revolution in Turmoil.* Albany, New York: SUNY Press, pp. 99-117.

Ferraro, Vincent. „Dependency Theory: An Introduction. " July, 1996.
http://www.mtholyoke.edu/acad/intrel/depend.htm

Fesharaki, Fereidun. 1980. *Revolution and Energy Policy in Iran.* London: The Economist Intelligence Unit.

Field, Michael. 1984. *The Merchants: Big Business Families of Arabia.* London: John Murray Publishers.

Fox News. "Bush Visits Saudi Arabia for Talks With King Abdullah." January, 2008.
http://www.foxnews.com/story/0,2933,322467,00.html

Frank, Andre Gunder. 1979. *Dependent Accumulation and Underdevelopment.* New York: Monthly Review Press.

Frimpong-Ansah, Jonathan. 1992. *The Vampire State in Africa: The Political Economy of Decline in Ghana.* Trenton: Africa World Press.

Gary, I. and T. Karl. 2003. *Bottom of the Barrel: Africa's Oil Boom and the Poor.* Baltimore, Maryland: Catholic Relief Services.

Gasiorowsky, Mark. 1987. "The 1953 Coup D'etat in Iran," in *International Journal of Middle East Studies*, vol. 19, pp.261-286.

Gause, Gregory.1994. *Oil Monarchies: Domestic and Security Challenges in the Arab Gulf States.* New York: Council on Foreign Relations.

Geddes, Barbara. 1994. *Politician's Dilemma.* Berkeley: University of California Press, 1994.1999a. "What Do We Know about Democratization after Twenty Years?" In: *Annual Review of Political Science* 2 (1999), pp. 115-144.

Geddes, Barbara.1999b. "Authoritarian Breakdown: Empirical Test of a Game Theoretic Argument." Presented at the annual meeting of the American Political Science Association, Atlanta, 1999.

Gelb, Alan and Associates. October 1988. "Oil Windfalls: Blessing or Curse?" In: *World Bank Research Publication.* Oxford: Oxford University Press.

Ghasimi, M.R. November 1992. "The Iranian economy After the Revolution," in *International Journal of Middle East Studies.*

Gheissari, Ali. 1998. *Iranian Intellectuals in the 20th Century.* Austin: University of Texas Press.

Graham, Robert. 1979. *Iran: The Illusion of Power.* London: Croom Helm.

Haggard, Stephan and Robert R. Kaufman. 1995. *The Political Economy of Democratic Transitions.* Princeton: Princeton University Press.

Herbst, Jeffrey. 2000. *States and Power in Africa.* Princeton: Princeton University Press.

Hiro, Dilip. 2006. *Iran Today.* London: Politico's Publishing.

Hodler, R. 2006. "The curse of natural resources in fractionalized countries" in *European Economic Review* 50: 1367-1386.

Hooglund, Eric. 1982. *Land and Revolution in Iran, 1960-1980.* Austin: University of Texas Press.

Human Rights Watch.1999. *The Iranian Legal Framework and International Law.* http://www.hrw.org/reports/1999/iran/Iran99o-03.htm

Human Rights Watch.1999. *The Price of Oil: Corporate Responsibility and Human Rights Violations in Nigeria's Oil Producing Communities.* www.hrw.org/advocacy/corporations/index.htm.

Ikenberry, John. 1986. "The Irony of State Strength: Comparative Responses to the Oil Shocks in the 1970s." In: *International Organization*, vol. 40/1, pp. 105-137.

International Monetary Fund (IMF).1979 to 1992. *Direction of Trade Statistics.* Washington.

International Monetary Fund (IMF). 2007. *Iran Country Report.* www.imf.org

International Monetary Fund (IMF). 2007.*World Economic Outlook Database.* www.imf.org

Iran Chamber Society. 2008. *The Structure of Power in Iran.* www.iranchamber.com

Isham, J., L. Pritchett, M. Woolcock,G. Busby. 2003. “The varieties of rentier experience: How natural resource export structures affect the political economy of economic growth,” in *Middlebury College Working Paper Series 0308*, Middlebury College, Department of Economics.

Issawi, Charles and Yeganeh, Mohammed.1962. *The Economics of Middle Eastern Oil.* London, pp. 105-6 and Table 30.

Karl, Terry. 2007. “Oil-led Development: Social, Political, and Economic Consequences,” in *CDDRL Working Papers.* Stanford University. http://cddrl.stanford.edu/publications/oilled_development_social_political_and_economic_consequences/

Karl, Terry.1997. *The Paradox of Plenty: Oil Booms and Petro-States.* Berkeley: University of California Press.

Karsh, Efraim. 1989. *The Iran-Iraq War.* New York: St. Martin’s Press.

Karshenas, Massoud.1990. *Oil, State, and Industrialization in Iran.* Cambridge: Cambridge University Press.

Karshenas, Massoud. 1998. “Structural Adjustment and the Iranian Economy,” in N. Shafi (ed.) *Economic Challenges Facing Middle Eastern and North African Countries-Alternative Features.* Basingstoke and London: Macmillan Press.

Katouzian, H.1978. “Oil versus Agriculture: a Case of Dual Resource Depletion in Iran,” in *Journal of Peasant Studies*, pp. 347-369.

Katzman, Kenneth. July 20, 2001. “The Iran-Libya Sanctions Act (ILSA),” in *Library of Congress, Washington D.C. Congressional Research Service.* http://stinet.dtic.mil/oai/oai?&verb=getRecord&metadataPrefix=html&identifier=ADA475995

Kazemi, Farhad. 1996. “Civil Society and Iranian Politics,” in Augustus Richard Norton, *Civil Society in the Middle East*, vol. 2. New York: E.J. Brill.

Keddie, Nikki. 1981. *Roots of Revolution: An Interpretive History of Modern Iran.* New Haven: Yale University Press.

Keshavarzian, Arang. 2007. *Bazaar and State in Iran.* Cambridge: Cambridge University Press.

Khan, Mushtaq and Jomo Kwame Sundaram, eds. 2000. *Rents, Rent-Seeking and Economic Development: Theory and Evidence in Asia.* Cambridge: Cambridge University Press.

Kheirabadi, Masoud. 1991. *Iranian Cities: Formation and Development*. Austin: University of Texas Press.

Khoury, Philip S. and Joseph Kostiner.1990. *Tribes and State Formation in the Middle East.* Berkeley: University of California Press.

Klapp, Merrie Gilbert. 1987. *The Sovereign Entrepreneur: Oil Policies in Advanced an Less Developed Capitalist Countries.* Ithica: Cornell University Press.

Krueger, A.O. 1974. "The Political Economy of the Rent-seeking Society" in *American Economic Review* 64 (3).

Ladjevardi, Habib. 1985. *Labor Union and Autocracy in Iran.* Syracuse, New York: Syracuse University Press.

Lewis, Bernard. 1988. *The Political Language of Islam.* Chicago: The University of Chicago Press.

Lewis, Bernard. 2003. *The Crisis of Islam.* New York: Modern Library.

Locke, John. 1980. "Of Property" in *Second Treatise of Government.* Indianapolis: Hacket Publishing Company.

Looney, Robert E. 1982. *Economic Origins of the Iranian Revolution.* New York: Pergamon.

Luciani, Giacomo.1988. "Economic Foundations of Democracy and Authoritarianism: The Arab World in Comparative Perspective." In: *Arab Studies Quarterly*, Vol. 10/4, pp. 457-475.

Luciani, Giacomo.1990 (ed.) *The Arab State.* London: Routledge.

Luciani, Giacomo.1990. "Allocation vs. Production States: A Theoretical Framework." In: Giacomo Luciani (ed.), *The Arab State.* London. pp. 65-84.

Luciani, Giacomo.1994. "The Oil Rent, the Fiscal Crisis of the State and Democratization." In: Ghassan Salamé (ed.), *Democracy Without Democrats? The Renewal of Politics in the Muslim World.* London: I.B.Tauris. pp. 130-155.

Luciani, Giacomo.1995. "Resources, Revenues, and Authoritarianism in the Arab World: Beyond the Rentier State?" In: Brynen, Rex, Bahgat Korany, and Paul Noble (eds.), *Political Liberalization and Democratization in the Arab World, Vol. 1, Theoretical Perspectives.* Boulder: Lynne Rienner. pp. 211-227.

Mahdavy, Hossein.1970. "The patterns and problems of economic development in rentier states: the case of Iran." In: *M. A. Cook (ed.), Studies in the Economic History of the Middle East.* London: Oxford University Press. pp. 428-467.

Margolis, Eric. June 19, 2007. "The Mother of all Scandals."
http://www.lewrockwell.com/margolis/margolis79.html

Marx, Karl .1867. *Das Kapital, Kritik der politischen Ökonomie.* Paderborn: Voltmedia.

Marx, Karl, Friedrich Engels and Robert C Tucker. 1986. *The Marx-Engels Reader.* Cambridge: Cambridge University Press.

Mayer, Ann Elizabeth. 1998. *Islam and Human Rights: Traditions and Politics.* Boulder, CO: Westview Press.

McDaniel, Tim. 1991. *Autocracy, Modernization, and Revolution in Russia and Iran.* Princeton: Princeton University Press.

McLachlan, K.S. and F. Ershad (eds.). 1989. *International Migration in Iran*. London: SOAS.

Menashri, David. 1990. *Iran: A Decade of War and Revolution*. New York: Holmes and Meier.

Mernissi, Fatima. 1987. *Beyond the Veil: Male-Female Dynamics in Modern Muslim Society.* Bloomington: Indiana University Press.

Migdal, Joel. 1988. *Strong Societies and Weak States: State-Society Relations and State Capabilities in the Third World.* Princeton: Princeton University Press.

Milani, Mohsen.1988. *The Making of Iran's Islamic Revolution: from Monarchy t Islamic Republic.* Boulder, CO: Westview.

Ministry of Petroleum. *Annual Report*. Tehran, Iran, various issues.

Mofid, Kamran. 1987. *Development and Planning in Iran: from Monarchy to Islamic Republic*. Middle East & North African Studies Press.

Mohsenin, M. 2001. "The evolving security role of Iran in the Caspian region," in Chufrin, G. (ed.) *The Security of the Caspian Sea Region.* Oxford. pp. 166-173.

Molavi, Afshin. 2001. *The Soul of Iran*. B&T.

Moslem, M. 2002. *Factional Politics in Post-Khomeini Iran.* New York: Syracuse.

Mossavar-Rahmani, Bijan. 1981. *Energy Policy in Iran: Domestic Choices and International Implications.* New York: Pergamon Press.

Mottadeh, Roy. 1985. *The Mantle of the Prophet: Religion and Politics in Iran*. New York: Pantheon Books.

Murphy, Kevin, Andrei Shleifer, and Robert Vishny. 1993. "Why is Rent-Seeking so Costly to Growth?" In: *The American Economic Review*, vol. 83, 2, p. 409-414.

Najmabadi, Afsaneh.1987. *Land Reform and Social Change in Iran*. Salt Lake City: University of Utah Press.

Naraghi, Ehsan.1994. *From Palace to Prison*. Chicago: Ivan R. Dee.

Nitzan, S. 1994. "Modelling rent-seeking contests," in *European Journal of Political Economy,* vol. 10, pp. 41-60.

North, D.C. 1981. *Structure and Change in Economic History*. New York: Norton & Co.

Okruhlik, Gwenn. 1999. “Rentier Wealth, Unruly Law, and the Rise of Opposition: The Political economy of Oil States,” in *Comparative Politics*, vol. 31, no.3 (April), pp. 295-315.

Olson, M., Jr. 1965. *The Logic of Collective Action*. Cambridge, Ma: Harvard University Press.

Omid, Homa. 1994. *Islam and the Post-revolutionary State in Iran*. New York: St. Martin's Press.

OPEC. *Annual Statistical Bulletin*. Vienna, Austria, various issues.

Owen, Roger. 2000. *State, Power and Politics in the Making of the Modern Middle East*. London: Routledge.

Pallage, Stephane and Michel Robe. 2003. “On the Welfare Cost of Economic Fluctuations in Developing Countries,” in *International Economic Review*, 44, 2, pp. 677-698.

Perthes, Volker. 1995. *The Political Economy of Syria under Assad*. London.

Perthes, Volker. 2000. *Vom Krieg zur Konkurrenz: Regionale Politik und die Suche nach einer neuen arabisch-nahöstlichen Ordnung*. Baden-Baden.

Pipes, Daniel.1983. *In the Path of God: Islam and Political Power*. New York.

Plan and Budget Organization. 1988. *A Summary Report on the Performance of the First Five-Year Economic, Social and Cultural Development of the Islamic Republic of Iran* (1989-93). Tehran: Plan and Budget Organization.

Polanyi, Karl. 1957. *The Great Transformation*. Boston: Beacon Press.

Qatar Country Report 2007. www.bayernlb.de/ar/Internet/en/Downloads/0100_CorporateCenter/5700Countries/CountriesL-Z/Qatar/E-Qatar.pdf

Rahnema, Saeed and Sohrab Behdad (eds.) 1995. *Iran After The Revolution: Crisis Of An Islamic State*. London and New York: I.B. Tauris.

Razavi, Hossein and Firouz Vakil. 1987. *The Political Environment of Economic Planning in Iran, 1971-1983: From Monarchy to Islamic Republic*. Boulder, CO: Westview.

Reiss, David. 2006. „On the Theory of the Social Revolution Reconsideration of a Marxian Prediction," in *Marxist Internet Archive*.
http://marx.org/history/international/comintern/sections/britain/periodicals/communist_review/1922/07/soc_rev.htm

Reissner, J. 2005. “Irans neue Distanz zum Westen,“ in *SWP-Aktuell 32*. Berlin.

Ricardo, David. 1821. *The Principles of Economy and Taxation*. London: Everyman’s Library.

Richards, Alan and John Waterbury. 1996. A *Political Economy of the Middle East.* Colorado: Westview Press.

Rodinson, Maxime. 1978. *Islam and Capitalism*. Austin: University of Texas Press.

Ross, Michael L. 2001. “Does Oil hinder Democracy?” In: *World Politics*, vol. 53/3, pp. 325-361.

Ross, Michael. 2001. *Extractive Sectors and the Poor*. Oxfam America Report. London.

Roy, Olivier. 1994. *The Failure of Political Islam*. Translated by Carol Volk. London: I.B. Tauris.

Sachs, J. and A. M Warner. 2001. “The curse of natural resources,” in *European Economic Review 45*, pp. 827-838.

Saikal, Amin. 1980. *The Rise and Fall of the Shah*. Princeton: Princeton University Press.

Samuels, W.J. and N. Mercuro. 1984. “A Critique of Rent-seeking Theory” in *Neoclassical Political Economy: The Analysis of Rent-seeking and DUP Activities.* Cambridge, Massachusetts: Ballinger Publishing Company.

Schatzberg, Michael G. and William Zartman, eds. 1986*. The Political Economy of Cameroon.* New York: Praeger.

Schmid, Claudia.1991. *Das Konzept des Rentier-Staates.* Münster: Demokratie und Entwicklung.

Schneider, Steven. 1983. *The Oil Price Revolution.* Baltimore: John Hopkins.

Schlumberger, Oliver. 2000. “Arab Political Economy and the European Union’s Mediterranean Policy: What Prospects for Development?” In: *New Political Economy*, vol. 5/2, pp. 247-268.

Schumpeter, J.A. 1994. *Capitalism, Socialism, and Democracy.* London: Routledge.

Seers, Dudley. 1964. “The Mechanism of an Open Petroleum Economy,” in *Social and Economic Studies*, vol. 13.

Shadpour, K. 1994. *The PHC Experience in Iran*, English ed. Tehran: UNICEF.

Sharabi, Hisham.1988. *Neopatriarchy. A Theory of Distorted Change in Arab Society.* Oxford: Oxford University Press.

Shaw, E. 1973. *Financial Deepening in Economic Development*. New York: Oxford University Press.

Shihab, Mohamed. 2001. "Economic Development in the UAE" in al Abed, Ibrahim and Hellyer, Peter (ed.) *The United Arab Emirates: A New Perspective*. Trident Press.

Siddiqi, Ahmad. 2004. „Khatami and the search for Reform in Iran," in *Stanford Journal of International Relations.*
http://www.stanford.edu/group/sjir/6.1.04_siddiqi.html

Simpson, John. 1988. *Inside Iran: Life under Khomeini's Regime*. New York: St. Martin's Press.

Skocpol, Theda. 1979. *States and Social Revolutions*. New York: Cambridge University Press.

Smith, Adam. 1960. *The wealth of nations* (1776). London: Everyman's Library.

Smith, Benjamin. 2004. "Collective Action with and without Islam: Mobilizing the Bazaar in Iran," in *Islamic Activism: A Social Movement Theory Approach* (edited by Quintan Wiktorowicz). Indiana: Indiana University Press.

Smith, Benjamin. Winter 2006. "The Wrong Kind of Crisis: Why Oil Booms and Busts Rarely Lead to Authoritarian Breakdown," in *Studies in Comparative International Development*, vol. 40, no. 4.

Smith, Benjamin. 2007. *Hard Times in the Lands of Plenty: Oil Politics in Iran and Indonesia.* Ithaca, NY: Cornell University Press.

Taleqani, S.M. 1982. *Islam and Ownership*. Lexington: Mazda Press.

The Economist. 2007. *Country Briefings Iran: Economic Structure.*
http://www.economist.com/Countries/Iran/profile.cfm?folder=Profile-Economic%20Structure

Tilly, Charles. 1990. Coercion, Capital and European States, AD 990-1990. Oxford: Basil Blackwell.

Torvik, R. 2002. "Natural resources, rent-seeking and welfare," in *Journal of Development Economics* 67, pp. 455-470.

UNICEF. 2007. *Division of Policy and Planning, Strategic Information Section*.
www.childinfo.org

Valadkhani, A. 2001. "An Analysis of Iran's Third Five-Year Development Plan in the Post-Revolution Era (2000-2005)," in *Journal of Iranian Research and Analysis*, 17(2).
http://ro.uow.edu.au/commpapers/399

van de Walle, Nicolas. 2001. *African Economies and the Politics of Permanent Crisis, 1979-1999*. New York: Cambridge University Press.

Vatikiotis, P.J. 1997. *The Middle East: From the End of Empire to the End of the Cold War*. London: Routledge.

World Bank.1979 to 1992. *World Development Report*. Washington.

World Bank. 1994. *World Development Report: Infrastructure for Development.* Oxford: Oxford University Press.

Wright, Robin. 2001. *The Last Great Revolution: Turmoil and Transformation in Iran.* New York: Vintage.

Yates, Douglas. 1996. *The Rentier State in Africa*. Trenton, N.J.: Africa World Press.

Zubaida, Sami. 1988. *Islam, The People and The State*. London: Routledge.

Glossary

Ansar-e Hezbollah: (lit.) "Helpers of Hezbollah"; the Ansar-e Hezbollah refers to an Islamist, militant group whose ideology is devoted to the velayat-e faqih, Ayatollah Khomeini's principles, and the eradication of foreign, non-Islamic influences.

Artesh: Iranian army

Basij: (lit.) "mobilization"; volunteer based Iranian paramilitary force founded in 1979. They are engaged in activities including law enforcement, emergency management, social services, etc.

Bazaar: (lit.) "marketplace"

Bazaari: the term "bazaari" refers to members of the Iranian bazaar, or marketplace, which constitutes an important socio-economic faction that played a significant role in the overthrow of the Pahlavi monarchy in 1979.

Bonyad: religious foundations established by the state to provide charities for the poor and needy.

Bonyad-e Mostazafan: (lit.) "Foundation for the Oppressed"; one of the most prominent religious parastatal foundations in the Islamic Republic of Iran.

Bonyad-e Shahid: (lit.) "Martyr's Foundation"; another prominent religious foundation, providing services and charities for the families of those killed in combat.

Ejtehad: (lit.) "authority"

Faqih: religious jurisprudent

Komitehs: (lit.) "committees"; committees set up by Ayatollah Khomeini's supporters after the Islamic revolution that served to consolidate clerical authority by mobilizing their power base throughout the country.

Majlis: Iranian parliament

Majlis-e Khebregan: (lit.) "Assembly of Experts";

Marja-e Taqlid: (lit.) "Source of Emulation"

Mostazafan: (lit.) "oppressed"

Mujahedin-e Khalq Organization (MKO): Iranian political party that follows the combined ideological principles of Marxism and Islam. Has conducted terrorist attacks against the clerical establishment of Iran in the past and advocates their overthrow.

Rahbar: (lit.) "leader"

Sayyid: a religious title bestowed upon males accepted as descendants of the Islamic prophet Muhammad.

Sepah: Iranian Revolutionary Guards

Tudeh: Iranian Communist party

Velayat-e Faqih: (lit.) “Rule of the Jurisprudent”

Made in the USA